Only The BEST

ON

CUSTOMER SERVICE

Great ideas for improving your life and your
business from some of America's top speakers,
trainers, consultants, and authors.

SHEP HYKEN • SUE HERSHKOWITZ • KEITH HARRELL • MIKKI WILLIAMS

DAN CLARK • VIC OSTEEN • SCOTT MCKAIN • LISA FORD • MEL KLEIMAN

ROXANNE EMMERICH • SUE PISTONE • MARC HARDY • LARRY WINGET

ONLY THE BEST

ON

CUSTOMER SERVICE

compiled by

Larry Winget

Copyright © MCMXCVI

Printed in the United States Of America.

Cover design and layout by Ad Graphics, Tulsa, Oklahoma.

Library of congress Catalog Number: 96-061319

ISBN:1-881342-13-1

"Only The Best ™" is a trademark of Win Publications!, Win Seminars!, and Larry Winget, denoting a series of books and other products that may include but is not limited to pocket cards, calendars, audio cassettes and videotapes.

Published by:

Win Publications!
a subsidiary of Win Seminars!, Inc.
P. O. Box 700485
Tulsa, Oklahoma 74170
918 745-6606

Addtional copies of
Only The Best On Customer Service
can be obtained from any of the authors by calling their individual number as listed with their chapter.

Quantity discounts are available.

All of the authors represented in
Only The Best On Customer Service
are members of the
National Speakers Association.

If you have an upcoming meeting and need a great speaker or even several great speakers then this book represents some of the finest in the business. Any of them would do an excellent job presenting an informative, entertaining keynote or seminar.

Please contact any speaker to recieve a full packet of materials explaining their speaking services and other products that may be available.

CONTENTS

1

Only The BEST

SEVEN WAYS TO CUSTOMER LOYALTY

BY

SHEP HYKEN

CUSTOMER SERVICE

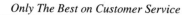

Seven Ways To Customer Loyalty

Shep Hyken

When I graduated college a friend came up to me after the commencement ceremony and asked me what I was thinking. I remember telling him, *"Wow, it is finally over!"* He then asked me if I knew the meaning of the graduation ceremony and of the word "commencement." Before I could answer he said, "This is not the end. Trust me when I tell you, my friend, this is just the beginning."

How right he was! Sage words for a young man coming out of college into the *real* world.

As I think back on this, I can't help but see the similarities between graduating college and the sales process. There is everything leading up to the sale, and then the sale itself. And that is just the beginning - commencement. Once the customer begins to do business, it is hopefully the start of a great relationship.

My friend, Dr. Larry Baker, says, "The most abused customer is the sold customer." This quote reminds me of an old story I once heard. It's one of those "a man died and went to heaven" stories. Now, don't worry, I'm not going to get religious on you. You don't even have to believe in Heaven , the Pearly Gates, or Hell. You don't even have to be a man! I think you'll get the idea.

A man died and went to Heaven. At the Pearly Gates St. Peter said, "We are doing things a little different than we used to. Even though you qualify for Heaven, you get a choice. You can stay here, or go downstairs to Hell. It's your choice and you can even spend a day in each."

The man spent that first day in Heaven and really enjoyed himself. It was quiet, relaxed and there seemed to always be soft harp music in the background. A nice serene and tranquil place to spend his eternity.

The next day he visited Hell. One of Satan's helpers showed him around. This was quite a wild place! Everybody seemed to be having one heck of a great time. They were drinking, dancing and having a ball. It was a non-stop party.

The next day the man was forced to make a decision. He visited with St. Peter and told him, "As much as I always thought I would end up in Heaven, those people down there know how to have a really good time. I've always been a little rowdy, so if it's no offense to you, I would rather spend my eternity down below."

"As you wish," replied St. Peter. With that, the same man that showed him around Hell yesterday appeared and he was ushered downstairs where he was immediately taken to a brick cell and shackled to the wall.

"It is here you will spend your eternity," the man was told.

The man cried out, "Wait, you can't do this! Yesterday when I was here everybody was partying and having a good time. What happened?"

The little devil turned around and replied, *"Yesterday you were a prospect. Today you are a customer."*

This short chapter is about the exact opposite of the above story. Once a person becomes a customer, the *service* side of the equation kicks in. Knowing how to keep existing customers happy is a key ingredient to the success of your company as well as your career.

Dr. Ted Levitt, senior professor at Harvard Business School says that the function of every business is to get and *keep* customers. Consequently, it is also the function of every employee of every business to do the same. Keeping customers long-term is key to the success of virtually every business.

No one has argued with the statement that it is much more expensive to attract new customers to a business than to keep existing ones. Every study and survey seems to prove this true. Depending on which studies you read, it can cost, on average, four to six times more to attract the new customer than to keep the existing one. So the importance of customer loyalty becomes obvious.

How can we build customer loyalty - to get that customer to come back again and again? As long as the product or service you and your company sell does what it is supposed to do and keeps up with (if not stays ahead of) the competition, it should be easy. Add to that the element of outstanding service, and customer loyalty takes place. Here are seven universal points that will apply to any type of business.

1. ***Don't ever forget to say THANKS!*** It can be face to face, over the phone or via written thank you notes. Customers like to feel appreciated. Recently I bought some clothes from a local retail store. Just a few days later I opened my mail and found a thank you note from my salesman. Was I impressed? You bet. Will I go back? You bet. And, when I do, I will be looking for *my* salesman.

2. ***Find out if you are doing a good job, and if there are problems react quickly.*** By the way, your customers will likely not tell you if there are problems. Numer-

ous studies have shown that complaining customers don't complain. TARP (Technical Assistance Research Program) was commissioned by the White House Office of Consumer Affairs to survey customer satisfaction. They found that an average business only hears from 4% of unhappy customers. The other 96% don't complain - at least not to the places they did business. While the study was conducted a number of years ago, current independent studies are still showing similar findings. Your ultimate goal should be to try and find any problems *before* the customer complains. The best way is for *you* to simply ask how you are doing.

3. *Make sure the customer knows they made the right decision to do business with you.* Educate and reinforce that they have made a good choice. If you do something different than the competition, make sure the customer knows about it. I remember buying meat from a grocery store. The butcher proudly held up the steak he was selling me and said, "Look at that! Is that a beautiful piece of meat or what? Did you know that we trim the fat around the steak to just 1/8 of an inch? You won't find that at the competition! Thanks for shopping with us." These competitive differences need to be emphasized. It is your opportunity to stand out.

4. *Guarantee your products and/or services.* Personally stand behind everything you do. A customer doesn't

do business with a company. They do business with the people who represent the company. And, make sure the customer knows you mean it. If there is a problem, don't just push it off to someone else, better referred to as the *It's Not My Department* reaction. If a customer has a problem, and you are the person that received the information, it is your responsibility to see it through. You may not make the final decision, but you are there when it is made. You may not actually fix whatever it is that might need fixing, but you are the last person the customer talks to after it is fixed. For example, I may check into a hotel. When I get to my room I find that the nightstand light is burned out. On my way out of the hotel to dinner I tell the front desk manager about the problem. The manager tells me that it will be taken care of. Now, do you think the manager is going to go up to my room to change a light bulb? I doubt it. But, this manager will call the maintenance department and ask them to do it. And afterwards, the manager will call my room to leave a message that the nightstand light has been fixed and to call if there are any other problems. He took responsibility for my problem.

5. *Recognize that there may be others in the "buying process" that should be made to feel appreciated.* Others may also be involved in the buying process, such as an assistant, a secretary or even a committee, but may not be the person or people you are dealing with. Or

maybe it is just a bystander. Not too long ago I bought my wife a piece of jewelry. I ventured out one Saturday morning with my six year old son, Brian. He wasn't very excited about going to a jewelry store, that is until the salesperson gave him a small toy airplane. You know the kind, a couple of pieces of thin balsa wood that fit into each other to form what looks like an airplane. This probably cost the store less than a quarter, but to say Brian was excited was an understatement! As a matter of fact, he can't wait to go back to that jewelry store again. He made it clear that if I ever bought anything for my wife, Cindy, I should always go back to that store. They make him feel special.

6. *Create a demanding customer.* Now, here is an interesting concept. Creating a demanding customer means that if your customer were to go to your competition, they would not just expect, but demand, the same level of service that they get from you. Anything less from the competition reinforces that the customer made the right choice to do business with you. In other words, you have spoiled your customer. What may be standard for you, is better than the competition. Just look at the first five of these six points. By doing all of the above the first time your customer buys your product or service, you will be on your way to exceeding their expectations. The only way a competitor can take your customer away would be to match or go beyond what you have done. If you have done all of the above, you

will have created a demanding customer and it won't be easy for the competition to steal him away. Customers get used to feeling special and being taken care of. The competition will find your customers not just demanding, but perhaps a bit unreasonable!

7. *Create Moments of Magic!* In 1986 Jan Carlzon, the former president of Scandinavian Airlines, wrote a book, *Moments of Truth*. In this book he describes the moment of truth as, *"Anytime a customer comes into contact with any aspect of your business, however remote, they have an opportunity to form an impression."* These points of contact are the moments of truth in business, and they can make or break you and your company. Carlzon says these moments of truth can be good or bad, and our goal should be to take every moment of truth, even if it is a bad one, and make it great. Turn every moment of truth into a *moment of magic!* Managing the moments of truth and creating moments of magic throughout the sales process, from the initial sales call to when the customer says yes, will help get you the sale. Creating moments of truth after the sale will help keep the customer *your* customer. Strive to make every moment of truth a moment of magic.

So there you have it. Seven ways for building customer loyalty. This is not just something to think about. This is something to do. You may or may not agree with all seven of these points, or you may feel the list is short and that there should be at least eight, ten or even more points. So add to it, change it or whatever. Just do it! Write them down and tape them to your desk. Look at them every day and don't ever let up on exceeding your customers' expectations. Work toward implementing them and you will find a higher success rate in keeping your existing customers for the long-term and creating MOMENTS OF MAGIC.

SHEP HYKEN

Shep Hyken, CSP is a speaker and author who has been entertaining audiences with his unique presentation style for 24 years. He has been hailed as one of the top entertainer/magicians working the corporate field. In 1983 he made the transition from entertainer to speaker. Hyken mixes information with entertainment (humor and magic) to create exciting programs for his audiences.

Shep Hyken has worked with hundreds of companies and associations ranging from "Fortune 500" size companies to smaller organizations with less than 50 employees. Some of his clients include American Airlines, Anheuser-Busch, AT&T, Fleming Foods, General Motors, Holiday Inn, Kraft, Monsanto, Shell Oil, Standard Oil and many, many more.

Main Topics Focus on:

Creating Moments of Magic, Excellent Customer Service, Customer Relations and Customer Retention — These presentations focus on how important service is in today's world. Make your organization a star in your customers' eyes. Some of the topics in these presentations include Jan Carlzon's Moments of Truth, Moments of Magic, parallels between selling and service, meeting and exceeding expectations, handling confrontations, building relationships and more.

Servicing Internal Customers — This is important to every employee of any business; from upper management to front line employees. Some of the areas discussed include the concept of the internal customer, management's new responsibilities and building better relationships. The front line may service, sell and have the most contact with the "outside" customer, but the internal people serve everyone else in the organization. Servicing and treating fellow employees like customers will have a direct positive effect on your organization's customer service/satisfaction program. Teamwork concepts can also be brought into this program.

You Are The Magic! — This motivational speech combines humor, magic, information and motivation to create an exciting and enlightening presentation for all types of audiences. It is a fun program that can incorporate parts of Shep's service programs or can include topics such as personal excellence, goal setting, turning negatives into positives, teamwork and more. This is an outstanding program for banquets and special events.

Focus On The Customer - LIVE! — Perhaps your organization has held focus groups where customers are brought into a comfortable environment and asked questions. Imagine taking the focus group live, in front of your organization's executives, sales people, etc. Shep Hyken will host and facilitate a focus group in front of your audience. Shep will learn specific information about your business and industry, learn about your customers, and develop questions to ask them. But most importantly, Shep will open the session up for questions from the audience. Your people will be able to ask these customers virtually any questions they have ever wanted to ask - no holds barred! Shep encourages participation and keeps the program moving with high energy and his own brand of humor. (You might say this is a cross between Phil Donahue and Jay Leno!)

OTHER PRODUCTS

Moments of Magic — 158 page book $12.95
A clearly written, easy-to-read, easy to understand guide to customer service for any-one in any job. It is filled with information, techniques, and stories that will teach you to deliver excellent service to your internal and outside customers.

The Winning Spirit — 198 page book $16.95
Published in cooperation with the United States Olympic Committee, twenty experts wrote on "achieving Olympic level performance in business and personal advance-ments." Authors include Shep Hyken (Gold Medal Customer Service), Frank Mcguire, Don Hutson, Tony Alessandra, Jim Tunney, Les Brown and more!

Only The Best On Success — 198 page book $11.95
If you like *Only the BEST On Customer Service* you will love this book. Motivation and success are what this book is about featuring Shep Hyken writing on *You Are The Magic!* as well as other inspiring authors such as Roger Crawford, Mark Sanborn, Keith Harrell and more!

Only The Best On Leadership — 206 page book $11.95
The third in the *Only the Best* series focuses on leadership and features Shep Hyken's chapter on *The Top Ten Traits of Great Leadership*. Other authors include Larry Winget, Scott McKain, Keith Harrell, Dan Clark, and more!

Shep Hyken "Live" on Customer Service — 55 minute video $49.00
This video on customer service covers topics such as complaining customers, relation-ship skills, moments of truth and other important issues. This was taped in front of a live audience and combines information and entertainment (humor and magic) to create an exciting presentation.

Service: Creating Moments of Magic — 2 videos & workbook $99.00
A video *learning system* with a focus on internal and external customers. The workbook includes exercises that will *personalize* the information to the viewer's day-to-day re-sponsibilities. Additional workbooks are only $5.00 each. An outstanding tool!

Please add $4.00 Shipping & Handling
Mastercard and Visa accepted. Call regarding quantity discounts.

For a *free* laminated 4x8 inch card summarizing the important points
of this chapter on customer loyalty, or to get more information on
Shep Hyken's keynote presentations and seminars, please contact:

Shep Hyken
Shepard Presentations
711 Old Ballas Rd., Suite 215 • St. Louis, MO 63141
(800) 829-3888 or (314) 692-2200 • FAX: (314) 692-2222
E Mail: ShepardH@aol.com
http://www.hyken.com/

2

Only The **BEST**

THE REAL SECRET TO EXCEPTIONAL CUSTOMER SERVICE

BY

SUE PISTONE

CUSTOMER SERVICE

THE REAL SECRET TO
EXCEPTIONAL CUSTOMER SERVICE

SUE PISTONE

Aren't we are always searching for the secret, the answer, the magic formula of what it will take to keep customers? We've read the books, read articles, attended seminars, and even surfed the net for all of the latest research, information, topics and strategies. So what is the real secret to EXCEPTIONAL customer service? My experience has proven it is better TIME MANAGEMENT and ORGANIZATION!

Surprised? Consider this. What if you had the time to implement what you already know? Had the time to find ways to surpass expected customer service? Had the time to add value beyond the expected to your customers by sending articles on new trends in their industry or by giving them referrals? Had the time to take better care of yourself so that you could take better care of your customers? Were organized so you were not searching through stacks of papers looking for a scratch piece of paper you jotted that new customer's name on? Had one or two extra hours in your day to focus more on providing exceptional customer service? You would provide better service, wouldn't you? Of Course. You may be thinking, this makes sense. But how can I do it?

As someone with over 20 years of experience with teaching people to do this, I have found it means changing old behaviors and forming new habits. Yes, forming new habits takes time, and must be reinforced. Old behaviors are strong and hard to break. Yet, to deliver EXCEPTIONAL customer service, we must become better at time management and organization. Through constant and consistent daily attention, we will experience the sure rewards. Sound impossible? Let me help you by giving some examples of how others have succeeded and delivered ... EXCEPTIONAL customer service.

TIME MANAGEMENT:

My motto is Life is time...Make it count!™ Are you making your time count with your customers? Ask yourself, are you focused on today? Living in the now? Are you making each customer feel important and special? Are you showing that you really care? Regardless of whether you are working in the hospitality, retail, corporate, education, or service industry, the objective is to give each customer EXCEPTIONAL service.

The following story is a reflection of strategies I deliver around the country in my customer service seminars. Lisa works in a large department store. After the training, her employer now encourages her to take the time to implement the strategies they have learned. They say go the extra mile. They encourage each salesperson to take a few moments and send personal thank you cards to customers they have served during the day. Lisa sets priorities. There is always so much work to be done — that doesn't include working with customers — there is never enough time to do it. No matter how much merchandise needs to be put up, no matter how many racks need straightening, the customer is always the highest priority. Lisa knows this. This is truly exceptional customer service.

Here is another new behavior Lisa learned in the training and practices. She pauses and takes a deep breath before waiting on each customer. This gives her time to mentally break from what she is doing and focus on the moment. She has learned that a deep breath is a physical trigger to her subconscious mind to change her focus. Lisa learned to have eye contact, listen to the customer's request, understand their needs, and make them feel like they are the only person in the store at that time. EXCEPTIONAL! Wouldn't you like to be Lisa's customer? You would feel like she really cared about you and your needs. You would feel like this salesperson was there to be of service to only you. You would look forward to doing business with her and that department store again.

Maybe you have experienced someone like Lisa. Here is another story of someone who delivers EXCEPTIONAL customer service to me. Her name is Gary and she works at Neiman Marcus in Houston, Texas. We have a relationship, when I call, she has my merchandise ready when I arrive at the store. Neiman's has empowered Gary so that she can help me with my purchases in any part of the store. The salespeople who are experts in other departments give assistance to Gary when she needs more information about a product I am buying. Teamwork is effective time management and tells me I am a valuable customer. Better time management is necessary for Gary to give me exceptional customer service.

ORGANIZATION:

We've looked at better time management. Now let's see how being organized improves customer service. What it is like to waste hours searching through papers to find what you need? Cringe at the piles and piles of work to be done? Struggle to return messages but the telephone just keeps ringing? Agonize when you forget to delegate a customer's request? Worry when you have delegated a request but don't know if it has been done? You become frustrated, irritable and out of control.

Help! You say. How do I get in control and give exceptional customer service? The answer is through Amazing Organizational Strategies! Amazing? Yes, that is right! The strategies are amazing because they work when you implement them. For example, here are a few strategies:

- having an information book
- using a 1-31 filing system
- having a place for everything
- using a daily activity log
- having color coded subject files
- having color coded customer files
- having organization of computer work
- having a special project area
- knowing how to prioritize work
- working in bundles of time
- using voice mail
- using a contact management program

Sounds overwhelming? It isn't; it's letting go of old behaviors and forming new habits.

Here are two key organizational tips that will make a tremendous difference for you to deliver EXCEPTIONAL customer service. The information book and the 1-31 filing system.

The Information Book:

The information book is a 1/2" to 1" binder filled with sheet protectors. In the sheet protectors, keep information such as the most frequently called numbers, most frequently asked questions, a description of each employee's position, a check list of how to do each job, the mission statement of the company, and any other important information. An information book will benefit people who work in an office, out in the field, or in a store.

Here's another real experience. Tammy ordered new glasses, but her specific frame was on back order. Before the frames came in, Tammy moved. Fortunately, the store was a chain and had a store in the city where she was relocating. Wanting to make Tammy's move a little easier, the store transferred the order to the new location. Tammy called the store in her new location to check on her glasses. Michelle, a new employee, assured Tammy that the glasses were in, and she would hold them for Tammy to pick up. When Tammy arrived at the store the next day, Michelle was off and no one could find the glasses. Tammy left the store very upset and dissatisfied knowing that she would have to come back when Michelle was there to get her glasses.

If there had been an information book, Michelle would have known exactly where the glasses should be held until Tammy could pick them up. Since the information book has all pertinent information on how to run the store, it would have had a section on where "holds" are kept for the customers.

The information book is very valuable in delivering EXCEPTIONAL customer service.

The 1-31 Filing System

The second Amazing Organizational Strategy is the 1-31 filing system. This system helps us live in day-tight compartments. We only have today; therefore, we need to plan for the most important tasks for the day. You may ask yourself what does this have to do with customer service? Let me show you. Consider this. You are going through all of your stacks of paperwork. You are getting overwhelmed with all the things you have to do. A customer calls and needs something right away. Now you have to find what the customer wants. Or you get a call from an angry customer. You are not in the best mood yourself due to the overwhelming work that is waiting on you. You have to stop everything and deal with the customer. You're supposed to provide them the best service possible. But how can you do that? You are overwhelmed in paperwork! Frustration is building! You cannot find anything you are looking for! You stop, look at your desk and floor area, at all of the stacks of work that need to be done. All out in plain sight so you can see everything. You'd like to burn it as you burn! What's the solution? I have the solution for this clutter that is piling up all around you. The answer is using a 1-31 filing system.

The 1-31 filing system is where you keep your work

that needs attention each day. It eliminates all of the stacks you have at your desk. This system is made of 31 manila file folders, which are labeled 1-31 (a folder for each day of the month), and 31 red hanging folders. The 1-31 filing system goes in the filing drawer that you use most often. Each manila folder is placed in its own red hanging folder. Red because this is hot work to be done. Place all of the folders in the drawer. Go through each piece of paper, one piece at a time, and decide if you are going to take action on it. If you are; put it in the day you are going to take action. If not, file it in a customer file or a subject file, delegate it out, or throw it away. You will find this method helps you feel in control of the paperwork instead of it controlling you. This prevents action items from falling through the cracks, and leads to very satisfied customers.

Using the 1-31 filing system will enable you to take care of customer issues in a timely manner. It is also beneficial in customer service because it allows coworkers to take care of customers when you are away from the office. They will know exactly where you keep all of your paperwork.

Here's an example where the 1-31 filing system would help. One night Julie was working late at the office and a customer placed a very large order. In a hurry to close and get home, Julie put the order in one of the stacks. She would take care of this order first thing in the morning. When she got home that night, she discovered she had to leave town on an emergency. She left a message on Charlie's (co-worker) voice mail that there are several client orders on her desk. They must be sent out before noon the next day. The next morning Charlie came to work, checked his voice mail, and realized he had to do both his and Julie's work. He completed his customer order requests and then proceeded to Julie's office to do hers. He knew he was in trouble when he opened the door and saw stacks of papers all over the office. After much time wasted, he located the right stack; however, the noon deadline had passed. Another customer was going to be disappointed.

If Julie had used her 1-31 system, Charlie would have gone into her office, opened the file drawer at her desk and pulled out the file for today. In that file would be all of the paperwork Julie had planned on doing that day. Charlie could have quickly obtained the customers orders, filled them and had another satisfied customer. As an added benefit Charlie would be less stressed and be able to give EXCEPTIONAL customer service, too.

Better time management and organization is the real secret to delivering EXCEPTIONAL customer service. The information book and the 1-31 filing system are two helpful strategies my clients use and notice positive results.

Remember knowledge is not power — implementation of knowledge is power. Use this knowledge to provide EXCEPTIONAL Customer Service. Life is time...Make it count!™

SUE PISTONE

Sue Pistone is a Business Development Specialist with 20 years of experience in the Sales Industry and is known as a merited speaker and consultant to diversified companies. Sue is an expert at eliminating the daily disorganization that often keeps individuals and companies from achieving the success they deserve. Dedicated to "cleaning up America's businesses" through organizational tactics, her clients achieve results that include peace of mind, control and the ability to focus on that which is of primary importance. Sue excels at helping others develop a clearly-focused strategic plan aimed at bottom-line results through increased productivity and profitability.

Sue's speaking style reflects her special talent for helping others to realize their self-worth and develop their true potential. She is referred to as "The Encourager" a title that reflects her ability to leave individuals with the heart-felt knowledge that they can begin immediately to become who and what they choose to be, today, without waiting. As a speaker, her messages are inspirational, motivational, and informative, delivered with an enthusiasm that is both genuine and contagious.

Sue is personable, intuitive, and positive results oriented. By researching and studying everyday, Sue is able to better serve her clients. She has spoken to thousands of people and worked with hundreds of companies and corporations generating greater sales, more productive employees, and sharper clearer new images for the future.

OTHER PRODUCTS

The Organized You! 4 Audio Cassette Album with Workbook $59.95
Sue Pistone's Organized You teaches you a step by step process on how to organize your office in a fast, simple, and logical method. Enjoy being proactive versus reactive, experience less stress, and offer better customer service. You can also implement these strategies into your personal life.

Life Is Time... Make It Count! 4 Audio Cassette Album with Workbook $59.95
In today's hectic and fast-paced world, it is absolutely essential to develop a time management system for easy and effective day-to-day living. Learn time management strategies to manage your day.

Directing and Producing Your Life —2 Audio Cassette Album with Workbook $29.95
This program is designed to assist you in creating and building your future through strategic planning. The goal is to experience the joy and pleasure of your life's journey to success.

Your Journey to Success Single Audio $12.95
Through motivation and inspiration, you can feel great about yourself! Listen to Sue Pistone in a live presentation on how to begin Your Journey to Success.

A Rapping Good Day! Single Audio $12.95
A fun and upbeat way to begin and end each and everyday positively. You'll be snapping your fingers and saying "I'm Great, I'm Terrific, I'm the Best!"

The Golden Rainbow Song Single Audio $12.95
A positive attitude song recorded especially for young children so that they may begin and end each day positively.

Shipping/Handling: Add $5.00 for the first item
and $1.00 for each additional item.
To Place an Order,
Please call
Sue Pistone & Associates
at
1-800-409-ICAN (4226)

3

Only The BEST

WHAT ELSE CAN I DO?

BY

KEITH D. HARRELL

AND

RALPH BIANCO

CUSTOMER SERVICE

WHAT ELSE CAN I DO?

KEITH D. HARRELL & RALPH BIANCO

We have all played the role of customer and have witnessed poor, indifferent, and sometimes unacceptable customer service. As customers, the cause of this problem, whether it be poor management, lack of employee education, poor attitude, cost containment, etc., is academic. What is important, is to realize that today your customer has a choice- a choice to build partnerships with solution providers that understand their needs, industry and customers. It's a simple fact, organizations with a strong sense of customer service and value will flourish while marginal or neutral providers will simply not survive. *What else can I do?* is the attitude and behavior you must embrace to elevate your level of customer service today. In this regard, I urge you to focus on these four questions:

1. Who is your customer and what are their needs?

2. What is the world class standard of customer service excellence in your industry?

3. What strategies or course of action do you need to take to compete?

4. Are you willing to pay the price?

If you do not know the answers to these questions, my favorite phrase I utilize in my *Attitude is Everything* seminar, "Are you playing to win or are you playing not to lose?", is a more fundamental question that you need to address. If you're not totally committed and 110% focused on a *What else can I do?* attitude, you don't have to worry about the game- it's already over!

Your first strategy to improve your customer service is *exceed the needs and expectations* of your customer. How is it that Nordstrom, one of the premier retailers in the country expands profitably, while their competitors struggle and falter; Microsoft, the leading supplier of personal computer software in the world, continues to gain market share and dominate the industry; FedEx ships more overnight documents and Starbucks serves more coffee than any of their competitors? Because they each clearly understand and execute a continuous *improvement* plan in exceeding the customers needs and expectations. To emulate these industry leaders and their success, you need to do the same. What is it about these companies and their culture that enables them to understand and consistently apply these strategies? Quite simply, a *What else can I do?* level of customer service.

What else can I do? levels of customer service can be experienced in every industry. The pilot of a major airline leaves the cockpit to discuss with his first-class customers why there is a delay in takeoff. He assures the first-class customers that all connecting flights will be met, despite the delay. Later, he repeats this information over the intercom for all other passengers. Realizing a dinner did not meet customer expectations, the general manager of a popular local restaurant appears at the customer's home the following day with a cash refund as well as a dinner certificate for two. When a prospective customer asks for directions, a gas station attendant not only determines the address and phone number of the destination, but provides a detailed map. This type of *What else can I do?* customer service begins and ends with *people-* people's attitudes- knowing that they *can* and *do* make the difference.

Premier customer service also requires a leadership strategy. Management must understand that retaining a customer is far less costly than marketing and selling to new ones. In other words, return-on-investment and profitability are directly linked to that service level required to ensure that your customer today is not your competitor's tomorrow. Additionally, this service level is a moving target: excellent service today is superseded by superlative service tomorrow as competitors continue to respond and "raise the bar". Astute managers of market leaders understand this phenomenon and realize that making a commitment to customer service requires an investment in both the infrastructure and work force to make service excellence a reality. This goes back to my question: "Are you willing to pay the price?" By investing substantial capital in leading-edge computer technology, Charles Schwab, the leading discount stock brokerage house, paid the price and is now able to provide their customers faster and less expensive stock trades than their much larger competitors. This provides Schwab the capability to provide a significantly higher level of service. The next investment is a vigorous employee training and education program that recognizes *everyone* as a service provider and is the primary on-going investment that will yield them significant dividends. In the final analysis, when employees are trained to efficiently and effectively respond to customers, and educated to understand that their actions and attitudes are ultimately the competitive edge, sales are made and profits are realized.

It is no coincidence that corporations with highly satisfied employees typically have highly satisfied customers. Employees with high morale are treated with respect, empowered to carry out their duties and responsibilities and are educated to focus on the customer. For example, Quality Food Centers (QFC), a Seattle based grocery chain, not only carries your groceries to your car, but will also shop for you and provide home delivery. QFC employees also provide advice on recipes, menus, are knowledgeable on various seasonal foodstuffs, and are empowered to make customer concessions in the checkout line when errors are made. QFC prices are also higher than their competitors, but with premier customer service and a *What else can I do?* attitude, price is not an issue. Home Depot provides one of the largest product inventories in the industry and has employees with the expertise to repair a roof, tile a bathroom, or install a home security system. QFC and Home Depot have much in common. They both sell commodity products. They both have well trained, motivated, satisfied employees. They both provide value, or at least the perception of value, to their customers. To a lesser or greater degree, the same could be said about many of their competitors, so where is the distinction? QFC, and Home Depot both have a fanatical obsession with customer service. This philosophy pervades their respective organizations and has become their mantra, their culture. Every employee is chartered with that common responsibility: *What else can I do for my customer today?*

While a sales representative at IBM I witnessed a *What else can I do?* attitude by an IBM receptionist named Doloris Brown. Doloris took personal responsibility and accountability by taking ownership of every customer call. A successful organization must have a strategy to empower every employee to be accountable, responsible and take ownership of every customer situation. IBM's annual sales quotas were traditionally allocated throughout the sales staff and each salesperson was expected to attain or exceed their individual quota. The truth is, the sales quota was allocated amongst <u>all</u> employees. When Doloris answered the telephone, the selling process or the opportunity to demonstrate exceptional service was underway. Whether it was a complaint, an order or a customer requiring general information, she took ownership and personally ensured the customers' needs were met. To simply greet a customer and connect them to the appropriate individual is only satisfactory today, and satisfactory is not indicative of premier customer service. *What else can I do?* Generate enthusiasm! *"I will connect you right away and I hope you have a fantastic day!"* When there is an on-site customer demonstration, *make it an event!* Provide the information in a complete and professional manner, *but make it fun!* Distinguish yourself from the competition so your customer will know you were excited and thrilled to have the opportunity. No matter what your position, when a customer complains, seize this as <u>the</u> opportunity to make it right. Involve management, but take personal responsibility for someone fulfilling your customers' needs in a *what else can I do?* attitude.

It is important to remember in today's competitive global marketplace, it is imperative that we, as corporations, small business and individuals provide leading-edge, premier, fanatical, obsessive customer service. The good news is that this is a highly profitable undertaking. It means increasing market share, retaining customers, and nurturing profits. The bad news is there is no alternative.

Competition is steadily raising the tide of customer expectations. Today's premier service level is tomorrow's norm. Customer service is the distinguishing factor among vendors as customers translate the service differential to value. In other words, in seeking the best value, customers will pay for a service differential. The key is to make the service differential apparent through a continuous process of improvement to customer service. *What else can I do?* will provide some answers in making that a reality.

There is no doubt that the pilot was demonstrating a *what else can I do?* attitude when he took the initiative and provided personalized service to his first class customers, or the general manager of the restaurant in going above and beyond in transforming a less than satisfactory experience into a memorable one, or the gas station attendant who took ownership of a potential customer situation and exceeded all expectations. The intrinsic value in these *what else can I do?* attitude examples is not in the isolated individual occurrence; it is in the collective experiences of multiple customers, who tell others, who in turn, tell yet others. Thus, a reputation is built and customer service is the delineating factor in the customers' vendor of choice. The question now is, what else can **YOU** do? to create an absolute level of extraordinary service to your customers.

KEITH D. HARRELL

Keith Harrell is a former IBM marketing executive and was one of their top training instructors with more than 13 years corporate experience. He has traveled around the world impacting the professional and personal lives of his clients. As a speaker, trainer, consultant, and author, Keith is highly recognized for his innovative and enlightening presentations. His high  level of energy, enthusiasm, and powerful messages are exhilarating. Keith's unique and charismatic style of delivery compels participants to take a "fix-it" or "kick-it" approach toward desired changes in attitude, increased confidence and productivity. Keith is described by his clients as dynamic, humorous and motivational.

RALPH BIANCO

Ralph Bianco is a consultant for Harrell & Associates, Ltd., who specializes in sales, marketing and management development. Ralph has a degree in business administration from the University of Notre Dame and has held various sales, marketing, and general management positions at IBM, The Boeing Company and Pacific Telesis. In addition, he has successfully established and developed national sales organizations for privately held firms and transitioned them into profitable, publicly held corporations. He has assisted many companies, particularly in the high-tech industry, in achieving their business objectives and sustaining controlled profitable growth while providing management training and consulting services.

OTHER PRODUCTS

Attitude is Everything: A Tune-up to Enhance Your Life. This best-selling book provides fundamental techniques to guide you towards establishing and maintaining a positive outlook that will enhance your personal and professional life $20.00

Attitude is Everything Audio Tape Series (2 tapes). This tape series includes highlights of Keith's live presentation that both educate and entertain 24.00

R.A.R.E. Opportunities (2 tapes). This newly released tape series focuses on change and discusses Realigning, Adjusting, Renewing and Enriching both your personal and business life 24.00

Attitude is Everything Audio Tape. Keith's most popular keynote address which includes practical tips on how to maintain a positive life-enhancing attitude. .. 12.00

Self-Confidence: The Key to Your Success Audio Tape. This exciting tape provides simple and effective techniques to enhance individual self-confidence 12.00

Change: The Power for Growth Audio Tape. Keith discusses change embracing versus change resisting and how to seize the opportunities that change present. 12.00

Attitude is Everything PC Screensaver. A Windows based screensaver that provides over 1,000 affirmations on enhancing your personal and professional life. 20.00

For more information or to order contact:

Harrell Performance Group, Inc.
4234 North Winfield Scott Plaza, Suite 103
Scottsdale, AZ 85251
(800) 451-3190 • (602) 423-5580 • Fax (602) 423-0526

VISA, MasterCard and American Express accepted.
Please add $5.00 for shipping and handling.

Please inquire about new soon to be released audio and video products.

4

Only The **BEST**

CUSTOMER SERVICE

OR

LIP SERVICE™

BY

MIKKI WILLIAMS

CUSTOMER SERVICE

CUSTOMER
SERVICE
OR
LIP SERVICE™

MIKKI WILLIAMS, CSP

Jay Leno once chided a supermarket clerk for failing to say thank you, and she snapped back at him, "It's printed on your receipt!"

I personally would prefer the warm smile and kind words of a person who genuinely loves their job and was truly happy to know that they had a significant role in making me a satisfied customer.

Customer service is like brushing your teeth—no matter how well you do it, you have to do it again and again…and often.

As a professional speaker and consultant, I have the opportunity to experience customer service do's and don'ts in a variety of venues—from all modes of transportation to all varieties of lodging, dining and through "customer service encounters of the strangest kind." Pun intended!

I have experienced Aha's, gained insights and yes, endured outrages when I would have preferred outrageous service.

Good service addresses the customer's perception and not always the reality. On a consulting assignment at an upscale health club, I overheard a member complaining to the Pool Director that the temperature of the pool was too cold. He replied that it wasn't and it was exactly the temperature it should be. At which point, the member became incensed as his opinion was devalued, and he was not "a happy camper." The director should have realized the member's perception was more important than the reality of the situation, by acknowledging his feelings, and offering possible solutions. These might be "I can appreciate how you feel, I can raise the temperature or I can suggest alternate usage times when the temperature is more comfortable and convenient. Ask for suggestions, collaborate on solutions or use humor to diffuse. The possibilities are endless and should be in sync with the companies service strategy, mission statement and visions and values. I have given Customer Service seminars from Senior Management to line workers, from South Africa to New York and in my experience, the organization's commitment to quality service is based on the value that is placed on it by the leadership, the comprehensive training and the hiring of the right people.

The Ritz-Carlton Hotels won the prestigious Malcolm Baldridge Award, one of this country's greatest achievement honors for customer service. Keith Beatty is the

Director of Human Resources at one of The Ritz-Carlton Hotels and a testament to their service philosophy. I met Keith when I spoke for SHRM (Society of Human Resource Management) at their annual convention and then he hired me to do a motivational presentation for his staff. From the greeting at the front door and throughout the hotel by passing employees, to the name recognition, the attention to service detail and the "attitude of gratitude" that permeates the hotel and it's employees, The Ritz-Carlton should be used as a model for all businesses. You don't have to be an upscale service provider to provide upscale service. Perhaps it is due to their Credo, part of which reads "The Ritz-Carlton experience enlivens the senses, instills well-being, and fulfills even the unexpressed wishes and needs of our guests" or their Three Steps of Service, or the 20 points that comprise The Ritz-Carlton Basics or their motto, "We Are Ladies And Gentlemen, Serving Ladies And Gentlemen." Whatever it is, this company has made a commitment to quality service and it is written, practiced, recognized and valued. While walking through the lobby on one occasion, I stopped a young dining room waiter, and asked for the nearest pay phone. Imagine my delight when he said, "Let me take you to it." What impressed me most was the employee empowerment towards guest satisfaction, uncompromising levels of cleanliness and friendliness and Keith's commitment to his internal, as well as external, customers. All great customer service organizations have visionary leaders like Keith.

The unexpected often creates what Ken Blanchard calls "Raving Fans." At a recent visit to the Adam Broderick Salon in Ridgefield, Connecticut, I completed my services and went to pay at the front desk. As the receptionist was looking over my "traveler" (salon lingo for the service and costs that "travel" with you from service provider to cashier), I was getting my money ready to pay and as I looked up at her to tell me the amount, she glanced back at my "traveler" and smiled and relayed this message, "Adam said, have a great day—no charge." Is it any wonder this magnificent looking salon won "Salon of the Year" and numerous other accolades? I'm not saying you have to "give away the store," it was the surprise element that was the WOW!

Our parents and teachers told us we learn by example so let me share some of my other WOW's with you that will hopefully inspire Aha's that will initiate, "I can do that."

I ordered a mattress for my Mom from Dial-A-Mattress and on delivery day, they were slightly behind schedule and called to ask if it would be too inconvenient to be two hours late.............and it was not. Within a day of delivery, I received the following letter;

Dear Customer: (would have been even better, had they used my name)

*It has come to my attention that your recent purchase from **Dial-A-Mattress** was delivered later than promised. Although there will always be unforeseen problems and mishaps, **Dial-A-Mattress** considers late deliveries to be a serious inconvenience to you our valued customer.*

Please accept our apologies and this $25.00 coupon, valid towards any future purchase of a premium set of bedding, etc., etc., etc.

After staying at the Irvine Marriott in California, when I checked out, I told the front desk receptionist how terrific the entire staff had been. She must have relayed this to the General Manager, and within a week, I received a <u>handwritten, personal note</u> from him, expressing his gratitude.

Customer service is the differentiating factor today in staying ahead of the competition. Ron Zemke said, "It's not how you manage the organization, it's how you manage the customer's experience with the organization." All things being equal, hotel to hotel, gas station to gas station, we must remember in customer service, a hotel is not just competing with another hotel. The health club I work out in today is being measured against the hotel I stayed in last night or the restaurant I dined in or the taxi I rode in. If I receive great customer service at that hotel, then my expectation level is high and my next service provider, be it the health club or my local cleaners will be expected to at least meet, if not exceed, those expectations. It's about expectations as well as perception. One of my favorite examples is the airline that starts the luggage belt before they even have the luggage. They realize that they can't possibly exceed expectations in this area so they are at least trying to meet them. When the passengers see the belt is moving they are happy thinking that the luggage must be on its way.

Whatever your business is today, it can and should evaluate what other businesses are doing to excel at customer service. Too often, companies are tunnel visioned and only look at their competitors in their field where much can be learned from outside your industry. Stew Leonard's the famous Supermarket in Norwalk, Connecticut profiled in countless magazines and books as the ultimate in customer service, prides themselves as the Disneyland of Dairy Stores and as such, created a Disney-like atmosphere with a live petting zoo outside for the kids, musical characters that sing in the store and WOW the Cow who walks around like Mickey at Disney. They didn't model themselves after another supermarket just because they were one but rather after a company like Disney, famous for their customer service, employee attitudes, and cleanliness. Even if you're a funeral parlor, be the Nordstrom's of funeral parlors, be the Ritz-Carlton of taxi drivers, be the Land's End of car washes, the American Airlines of computers..............adapt, adopt, model, learn from and create your own uniqueness and differential advantage as a customer service provider.

American Airlines sends its frequent flyers, "You're someone special" stickers so that whenever they get great service, whether on the phone with someone they haven't met or in person, they can give them a sticker which the employee can use to redeem great gifts. This idea has provided great inspiration to some of my clients in how to recognize employee efforts for giving great service.

Good customer service is not a cost, it is an investment and training your people to be the best service provider is the return on that investment—a satisfied customer. Anyone can copy your product and delivery—those are mere components of service—the unique factor is in developing a service mindset.

One of my careers was in the entertainment industry, where it's been said "all the world's a stage and everyone is a player" or in today's terms, when a Disney employee was asked how he liked being a street sweeper, he replied, "Oh, I'm not a street sweeper, I'm in show business, I'm part of the act". Make all of your employees part of a quality service team so they truly feel "part of the act."

When I returned to The Ritz-Carlton to give a half day training in teamwork, I couldn't help but notice the consistency of great service. How many times have you been to a restaurant and bragged about it to your friends and clients, only to return and be embarrassed by a marked difference in consistency and quality of service?

I called Tarala Electric in Norwalk, Connecticut when I was not satisfied with the electrical contractor who had been involved in the construction of my home. All of his technicians were always neat, friendly and efficient—the key words here are <u>all</u> and <u>always</u>. I found out later that Bill Tarala rewarded them in many ways from recognition trips to events that fostered teamwork. Two incidents stay with me in particular. Many of his electricians, while working in my home for a few years must have noticed that I collect lips. No, not real ones! Hey, some people collect butterflies, cars, stamps, I collect lips—lip phones, towels, magnets, I even have a lip toilet seat and 5 foot red lip couch. If you're wondering why, well, that's another book. Anyway—one day, I came home and noticed a gift wrapped package with a big red bow on my front porch. I opened it and found a framed graphic print of various shaped lips with a note that read, "We were wiring an art gallery, saw this, chipped in, thought of you. Enjoy. The guys at Tarala." WOW!

When I was building the house, I had a very large bill and very limited cash flow and when I called to ask Bill if I could pay it out, he replied, don't bother, just pay everyone else you need to and pay me when and how you can. No wonder I still use this company after <u>20 years</u> and refer them to everyone I know. Just like many of us in today's fast paced society, too many businesses look for the initial sale and forget about the long term relationship.

Then there was the time I was staying at a hotel in Boston and called to get driving directions. I asked for the Concierge and the receptionist said, "What room are they in?"

Or how about the time my driving service dropped me at the wrong airport. I missed my flight, had to take a taxi to the right airport, I lost time, money and was stressed to the max ,only to return home, expecting to find a note of apology, and possibly a free trip, when to my dismay, I received a bill and a follow up call blaming me. Needless to say, I never used them again and told as many people as I could. And folks, giving bad service to a professional speaker is worse than giving it to a mystery shopper, because we speak to thousands of people who might use your product or service. The point is you never know who that customer is and they should be treated with consistently awesome service.

Is everyone an expert at your business? Can they answer questions or will they ask me how to spell Concierge so they can look it up on the guest list? (She really did, I couldn't possibly make that up!) Is everyone empowered like they are at Nordstrom's department store, another icon of great customer service, where everyone is responsible for satisfying customers and you can shop to live piano music in the background. Is everyone trained, recognized and rewarded for great customer service experiences, not just sales? Do you provide training in personal and professional development so your employees have good communication skills? Creativity, problem solving, self-esteem, positive attitude, motivation, teamwork..........they all contribute to the overall success of a great customer service company. Technology may lead us into the 21st century ...... it can never replace the warmth of the human smile, the kindness of the human heart and the spirit of giving a joyful experience to another human being.

Don't forget to brush your teeth!

©1996 Mikki Williams Unltd.

MIKKI WILLIAMS, CSP

A Speaker Who Lifts You Up
&
Never Lets You Down

Mikki Williams, CSP, is an international speaker, trainer, author and consultant based in Westport, Connecticut. Mikki has spoken on every continent, earned her designation as Certified Speaking Professional (CSP), an honor bestowed on less than 300 professional speakers worldwide, won the National Speakers Association Golden Mike Award, presented at The White House, and President Mandela's South African home, the prestigious Million Dollar Round Table, she was featured on the front page of The Wall Street Journal and ABC did a television documentary about her life. She has nurtured nine entrepreneurial careers to personal and professional fulfillment. Her diversified business background spans several industries including retail, service, management, marketing, media, health/fitness, entertainment, hospitality and has given her a wealth of experience in business dynamics, personal growth and wellness. Her unique and inspirational life story touches the hearts and souls of people of all ages globally.

Mikki's diversified careers and life experiences have made her the focus of the media and, not surprisingly, The United Nations Outstanding Connecticut Woman of the Decade, The International Fitness Business Person of the Year, Entrepreneur of the Year and Small Business Advocate of the Year. She hosted her own weekly radio and television show and *customer-izes* all her presentations to clients such as IBM, Bristol-Myers Squibb, AT&T, and Lockheed. Her topics include motivation, teamwork, sales, presentation skills, customer service, marketing, business dynamics and personal and professional development. She gets rave reviews and standing ovations for her spectacular presentations. There is a fundamental humanness to her presentations, as she takes audiences through a life's worth of emotions and experiences incorporating her skills as a professional speaker, entertainer and humorist. An Enthusiologist™ who went from dance choreographer through nine successful careers to word choreographer, she mixes entertainment and humor with business savvy and knowledge to share insight and inspiration for life changing impact. From the corporate world to the ever changing world we live in, she is a breath of fresh air; outrageous, fun, stimulating, informative and most of all, real!

OTHER PRODUCTS

Pyromania: How To Set A Fire Under Yourself™ .... *(audio)* $15.00
Humorous, Inspirational Keynote – A catalyst for change .... *(video)* $50.00

Getting The Word Our™ .... *(4 audios)* $50.00
Low Cost/No Cost ideas to promote your business

"A Dancing Star" .... *(book)* $15.00
A book of inspirations to guide and heal.

Coping And Stress Profile $15.00
A unique learning instrument that focuses on stress and coping.

Time Mastery Profile $15.00
A powerful tool for self-assessing your time management areas of improvement.

Personal Profile $15.00
Discover your behavioral style and the environment most conducive success.

Carpe Diem (Seize the Day) mug $20.00
Thermographic: Changes to "Seize the Day" when filled with hot liquid.

Carpe Diem music .... *(tape)* $15.00
Performed by keyboardist: "A soundtrack for living" .... *(CD)* $20.00

"WYSIWYG" rhinestone pin $20.00
Adapted from computer jargon "What you see is what you get"

"You're A Smash"™ Tack pin $20.00
Glass jewelry that encourages risk taking.

Please add $5.00 Shipping & Handling

To order or for more information about Mikki's products,
speaking, training, or consulting services contact:
Mikki Williams Unltd.
40 Hermit Lane, Westport, CT 06880
V. 203-454-0770 • F. 203-221-7071
e-mail: mikkiwill@aol.com

5

Only The BEST

CUSTOMER SERVICE AIKIDO

BY

SUE HERSHKOWITZ

CUSTOMER SERVICE

CUSTOMER
SERVICE AIKIDO

SUE HERSHKOWITZ, CSP

If you offered my son a million dollars, I think he could not duplicate what had occurred by accident. He was eight years old and Champion, the puppy, was less than a year. The two of them were playing in the back yard. Michael was practicing his (miniature!) golf swing, using a rusty old golf club and a tennis ball. Boy and dog were having a great time until I heard the puppy yelp. Apparently, the ball had hit him right in the eye. When I examined the puppy, I couldn't see the pupil of his eye. I immediately called the vet.

The vet wasn't in. (Did I mention that this accident occurred about 5:00p on a beautiful Saturday afternoon?) "Hello," the vet's answering machine voice said at a pace slower than a turtle on its last legs, "You have reached the offices of Dr. Noname. We are not in at the moment. (No duh!) Our office hours are (they varied each day). If this is an emergency (finally!), please leave your name and number and I will return your call shortly."

I was frantic. At breakneck speed, I explained the story, left my name and number, and ran back to the puppy. Michael had put an ice pack on Champion's eye and when he lifted it for me to reexamine the situation, the eye actually looked kind of normal. A few minutes later, the eye looked fine (though a bit red) and the dog no longer wanted to be bothered with the ice pack, or with sitting still. He was ready to play again.

I consulted my son. "Do you think I should call the vet back and tell him it isn't an emergency?" Michael was relieved his dog was okay and he, too, was ready to play. "Nah," he said. So I took his advice and didn't call to cancel the emergency. It took almost two days - until Monday morning - for the vet's office to call to see if I wanted to schedule an appointment.

Okay, so maybe I overreacted. How was I to know a young dog's "normal" reaction to a direct hit to the eye? Obviously, the vet knew everything would be fine, but was that enough? How often do we serve the customer and yet not really serve their needs at all?

Of course, I no longer use that vet (and will gladly provide his name to anyone in the Phoenix/Scottsdale area!) but it got me thinking about the true meaning of customer service. How often do we, as vendors, sales people, real estate, medical or legal professionals, think we are providing efficient service and yet have no clue about our client's, customer's and patient's perception?

Is it possible to truly serve today's customer? In a global marketplace, can we provide the type of service that the customer/client needs, wants and is willing to pay for? You bet!

Blend Energy

As a yellow belt in the martial art of Aikido, I've learned that true control comes only by way of letting go and by not trying to resist or coerce the partner. (All opponents are considered partners. Think of the change in mindset between the words opponent and partner.) It's only through blending of energy that success can be achieved.

What does the customer want? To give you a hard time? Probably not! He or she simply wants his or her situation fixed. How can you do it without resistance? Determine how you can both win.

Booker T. Washington, a black educator, founded Tuskegee Institute in Alabama in the 1880s. One day he was walking past a plantation when the white mistress of the house, yelled for him to chop firewood. Professor Washington removed his coat, cut a pile of wood and carried it into the kitchen as she had asked. One of the servants recognized the professor and later told the mistress who she had cut the wood.

Embarrassed, the mistress visited Professor Washington in his office the next day. She came to apologize. "It's entirely all right, Madam," the professor said, "I like to work and I'm delighted to do favors for my friends."

How can both people win? Professor Washington's new friend became a true friend and worked hard to raise thousands of dollars for the institute.

Focus on what the customer needs to feel good about the situation and find a way to do it. Blend energy to gain cooperation and enjoy harmony, loyalty and delight customers.

Understand you have no control, and ultimate control.

A few years ago, I was keynoting a meeting of a worldwide floral delivery company. As I always do when presenting a program, I fax a dozen or so members of the audience prior to the program. I ask questions regarding their vulnerabilities and strengths and what they need to learn to make their time in the meeting worthwhile. Their responses, along with my other research of the client's needs, allows me to custom tailor my message to their specific objectives and provide significant ROI. One question I asked the floral group was: *What factors, outside of your control, have affected the way you do business?* One respondent wrote: "Domino's pizza."

Intrigued, I followed up with a phone call. "Domino's

Pizza," she said. "They've ruined our business. Now everyone expects that everything, including flowers, will be delivered within 30 minutes."

Yup. That's right. And as a floral service provider, you have two options: You either educate your consumer or you deliver flowers within 30 minutes.

The reality is that expectations change and are progressive and you have absolutely no control over any factors. What is the only thing you have absolute control over? It's the way you respond to the new expectations and new realities.

Proactively, educate the reader. With each flower delivery, for instance, send a booklet detailing the steps to creating a personalized arrangement. In direct mail, include a brochure outlining the procedure. On the phone, explain when the flowers will be delivered. (Offer expedited service for a fee - after all you'll need to pull people off of other jobs.) Call the person who received the flowers the next day to see if everything arrived fresh and to their liking. Write a note to the sender (if appropriate) to thank them for their order - again explaining and educating about flower deliveries. Focus on becoming partners - not enemies.

Use the Disneyland school of thinking when promising when the flowers (or printing, or package, or proposal) will arrive. Have you ever stood on line at Disney? Remember what you pass on your way to that line? You pass a sign that tells you how long it will take to get to the attraction from that point.

And they lie. They lie in their guest's favor. If the sign says the line will take 30 minutes, you can set your watch that it will take less than that. (Think about it.. we're fine for those thirty minutes.. but at 31 minutes we become annoyed! They said 20 minutes - where's the manager of this thing?!)

One final point: Check your systems. Can you control the time it takes to deliver those flowers? Yes! Why? What can you do to achieve 30 minute delivery? It's quite possible that the benchmark other companies set for you will help you to control costs, time and service.

Manage Expectations

Your client or customer really wants to be a good customer. Sometimes they just don't know how. They read your brochure and you promise delivery within 24 hours. They read your advertisement and you offer an unconditional money back guarantee. You promise to do things bigger, better, cheaper for them. And then when the service is less than ideal, they complain. Hmmm!

Southwest Airlines offers a wonderful example of managing expectations. You board Southwest at your own risk... they provide no pre-assigned seating – only a numbered boarding card. When they're ready to board the plane, they yell out the numbers, and if you have that number you rush on board. (The closest barnyard sound I can think of to give you a clear picture of the feeling - and the boarding situation - is mooooo!)

Don't get on a Southwest flight without eating first. It doesn't matter if your flight is 30 minutes or three hours, you aren't going to see any food. You can have as many peanuts as you'd like, but food - as in a meal - no chance. They have no food galleys!

Southwest won't interline baggage either. If you fly Southwest form Phoenix to LA and then switch to Hawaiian Airlines to continue your trip, you must first go to the Southwest baggage carousel, pick up your baggage and then schlep it (hand carry) to Hawaiian Air.

Sounds like Southwest shouldn't be best of best in anything. Yet, for three consecutive years, Southwest beat out all competing airlines in every ranking and rating of both customer service and customer satisfaction. What? How?

Southwest manages expectations. They don't promise the moon and the stars and the sun. They promise cheap fares, fun service and on time performance. Period. Anything else is gravy - and because they are able to exceed our expectations, they enjoy passenger loyalty unparalleled in the airline industry.

Manage expectations by clearly communicating what you will do, when you'll do it and how it will be done. Help your customer be delighted with your services - not disappointed.

Understand What the Customer Pays For

Do you know what your customer/client really pays for? If you think it is the actual product you produce, you're probably way off base.

A few years ago I had the wonderful opportunity to speak on a program with Ron Pobuda. Ron said, "If Sports Illustrated magazine had understood they were in the sports information business instead of the publishing business, we would have the SI channel instead of ESPN." Wow! Think about it. It's not that SI is doing poorly -but what could they have been had they realized the service they were really providing their customer?

What service does the veterinarian provide? Sure, he or she is a medical expert, but do I know that? Can I tell if he or she does the right thing medically to my pet? Can the dog tell me if he or she prefers one vet's touch over another? What I pay for is peace of mind. What I need is a doctor who not only pays attention to my dogs medical needs, but to my psychological ones as well.

Jack Welch, CEO of General Electric, claims he will fire you if you say that what GE does is manufacture and sell large appliances like refrigerators and washing machines. Of course, what GE does is exactly that. But what business are they in? If they're selling refrigerators, they're in the food preservation business. Washing machines and dryers? Fabric care business. Think of the products and services that become solutions for GE to offer their customers.

What business are you in? Working with a group of real estate professionals, I asked that question. "Selling homes," most of them yelled out. "Yeah, that's true..but what business are you REALLY in?" Finally, someone yelled out, "Making dreams come true." What a difference that would make in the way they approach each customer, each prospect, each transaction. What business are you in?

I believe the business most of us are in is that of creating connections. Just as Aikido teaches it is more important to gain cooperation than to be right, those businesses that exist to serve their customers' needs - instead of their own - will survive and thrive.

Take Credit for the Service You Provide

The first time I brought my car back to the dealer for

a repair, I was amazed when the car was returned, not only fixed, but clean! No one had told me about this added service and I know it not only pleased me, it made the car run more smoothly. I must have told dozens of people about this extraordinary service.

Do I still think this service is outstanding? Well, it's nice, but it's a pretty expensive car wash you know (repairs are never cheap!) and sometimes, can-you-imagine-this, they actually miss a spot on the dash and I feel like asking them if they would run it through again. Okay, I admit it... I'm spoiled. But they spoiled me and they do nothing to remind me of the extra service they're providing. As far as I'm concerned, it's all become rather ho-hum.

What could they do? To begin with, each time the car is presented to me (yes, it should be a presentation for what I pay!), the person delivering it should say something like, "Your car looks great," or " Let me just polish this mirror for you, I see the car wash left it spotted," or "We washed and cleaned the inside today for you. Is there any trash in the trunk I could through away for you?"

An attorney friend of mine stopped charging clients for postage and copies. He figured his fee was high enough (I'd say!) to include the thirty two cents he was getting back! It was interesting though. He said that clients always complained about the additional charge on the bill but never said anything when he stopped charging it.

Guess what he didn't do? He didn't educate his clients. He assumed that they would all simply know and appreciate what he was doing. Wrong! I suggested he send a letter to his entire database explaining the new policy (not including the part about how high his fees are!). Second, I told him to include the actual costs on his bill, and then deduct it on each future invoice with the words "Complimentary Service."

As a professional speaker, I'll often have only a bagel and coffee for breakfast. My clients expect to pay for my travel expenses and they also pay a fair price for my speaking services. Why charge them $2.50 for my breakfast? If I need the $2.50 that much, I should really consider raising my fees. Like the attorney, we note on the invoice, "Breakfast - No charge," or "Worksheets - Complimentary." Had I simply eaten the costs (sorry about the pun), no one would appreciate that I chose not to charge them.

What services do you provide that both you and your customer take for granted? It's up to you to educate your client. If you don't point out what you do, it becomes no big deal (even when it really is.) Take credit for what you do.

The next time you have a customer service challenge, think about the Aikido way of delighting the customer. Breathe deeply, count to ten and then offer thanks for the opportunity to create a winning customer service experience.

SUE HERSHKOWITZ, CSP

Sue A. Hershkowitz has **spoken before more than three-quarters of a million people** both nationally and internationally during the past 14 years. Her corporate, association and government client list reads like a Who's Who of recognizable names, including: Walt Disney Studios, Marriott Hotels and Resorts, American Express, the US Navy and even the IRS! Sue has presented to associations such as the Young President's Organization, American Heart Association, American Society of Association Executives and has been **asked back by Meeting Professionals International twelve times!**

Sue holds a B.A. in English, a masters degree in Counseling and earned a **fellowship sponsored by the University of California at Berkeley.** Twice elected to the **Board of Directors of the National Speakers Association**, Sue currently serves on both the Executive and Finance committees. In addition, she has served on Meeting Professionals International **Meeting Manager** Editorial Advisory Board and the **Meeting News** Industry Advisory Board.

In 1993, Sue earned her **Certified Speaking Professional** designation. This recognition has been presented to fewer than

300 of the 3,300 National Speakers Association members. The C.S.P. signifies Sue's commitment and dedication to the speaking profession.

Sue's book, P*ower Sales Writing: What Every Sales Person Needs To Know to Turn Prospects Into Buyers!* is the **business building book** of the year! Everyone needs to communicate more powerfully and this book provides specific strategies and training examples to give readers the **definitive edge**.

Sue is known for her **content-rich presentations, fresh perspective** and her **energetic, enthusiastic** and **entertaining speaking style**. Her keynotes and workshops provide **practical, immediately usable** tools and techniques focused on empowering attendees to reach their professional and personal potential. Call Sue to jump start your next meeting!

Future Focus
- The Future is for The Open Minded
- Twisting the Familiar: Keys to Success, Profits and Sales
- "Magic Eye" Thinking: See the Possibilities

Customer Service
- Hyperservice™
- Service Doesn't Cost Extra!
- The Banana Peel Factor: How to Keep Your Customers From Slipping Out the Door!

Communications
- Power Writing
- You Think I Said What?
- Dealing with Crazy People - and Getting Results!

For more information on Sue's Keynotes and Intensive Training Workshops, please call 602•996•8864.

■ OTHER PRODUCTS

Power Sales Writing: What Every Sales Person Needs To Know to Turn Prospects Into Buyers! — 140 pages $15.95
Compel your prospects to read your message. Discover how you can grasp their attention within five seconds and save up to 80% of the time you now spend writing. If you communicate in writing, this book is a must-read.

The Banana Peel Factor: How To Keep Your Customers From Slipping out the Door!
Videotape - 60 Minutes $59.95
Understanding what service factors matter to your customers can make the difference between average service and legendary. This live presentation will keep you laughing as you learn how you can exceed customer expectations for greater loyalty and profits.

The Success Formula: How To Get the Results You Want!
Audiotape - 60 minutes $14.95
What can you do to reach your personal and professional potential? Find out how successful people master change, communicate more persuasively, and position themselves for success.

Dog Tales for the Heart — 208 pages — $9.95
A compilation of true stories to warm your heart and inspire your soul. You'll laugh and cry with the sweetness and unconditional love provided by our faithful companions. Real people and regular dogs together for an unbeatable combination of love, motivation and inspiration. Buy a copy for yourself and another to give as a gift. Every dog lover will treasure this book!

Please add $3.95 for postage and handling. Items will be sent two-day mail.

Special Offer
Order Power Sales Writing and The Success Formula and enjoy the customer service video, The Banana Peel Factor, for a 50% saving ($30.00).
Or
Order The Banana Peel Factor and select either Power Sales Writing or The Success Formula as our gift to you.

To order these products or to speak to Sue
about availability for an upcoming meeting, please call:
High Impact Presentations
14826 North 54th Place
Scottsdale, AZ 85254
V. 602-996-8864 • F. 602-996-6667
or
Hershk@aol.com   74117,56 @ Compuserve

6

Only The **BEST**

From The
Ground Up

By

Vic Osteen

CUSTOMER SERVICE

FROM THE

GROUND UP

VIC OSTEEN

It has been said that during the 70's businesses emphasized finance, during the 80's marketing, and in the 90's the emphasis is on Customer Service. Unlike finance and marketing, Customer Service must involve every aspect of the organization to be successful.

SOW IT DEEP

Customer service cannot be the program of the month and produce the desired results. It must be planted at the root of the organization, not merely applied to the surface to be successful.

Service must be established in the company's purpose. Not only service to the customer, but to all who are affected by the activities of the organization.

When I think of an ingrained service attitude, I am reminded of the slogan worn on pins by all employees at the Hard Rock Cafe. It states, Love all, serve all. Not love the customer and serve the customer, but ALL. This

ALL includes customers, suppliers, fellow employees and even management.

How do we achieve this type of attitude within the organization? First, incorporate people and a service attitude into your Mission Statement and Purpose. Write it down, put it on lapel pins, post it on your wall, use the service word often and it will become a part of the mindset of the organization. I love the purpose statement of Federal Express, a $5 billion cargo company, and the leader in the industry. It reads "People, Service, Profits." They believe that if you take care of the first two you cannot help but have the third.

SHOW UP

It is vital in developing a reputation for quality customer service to SHOW UP! Be there when you say you're going to, or be sure you communicate any change to your customer. I believe that if you do nothing other than this you will be wealthy. For some reason, there is a pervasive attitude that you can say you're going to be somewhere or do something and then just not be there and that's OK - they'll understand, people don't really expect you to show up anyway. Well, bull——. It is the over-promise, under-deliver ideology. When I was in the landscaping business, I can't tell you how many times I got the job at the price I asked only because I was the only one who came through when I was supposed to. People like it when you do what you say you're going to do. You build trust and loyal customers from the start.

JUST SAY NO!

We are taught that we need to do everything we can to make the customer happy, the customer is always right, that we want to please the customer at any request. Sometimes the best way to do that is to just say No!

Like it or not, we cannot be all things to all people. Often the best way to serve your customer is to honestly say no to them. What they request may not be profitable for you, or may compromise your policies or integrity and will cost you in the long run. This does not mean that you should not help the customer find what they want or need.

One retailer who I believe does an excellent job of training its people in customer service is Home Depot. I was doing some remodeling in my bathroom and needed a three screw C-clamp to attach formica to the counter top. I asked the service person if they had such a contraption. He walked with me over to the C-clamp area and we perused the boxes to no avail. He said, "No, it doesn't look like it, but let me call another store to see if they have one." I thought he was calling the other Home Depot. He quickly returned and said, "They have six of them at Swinneys Hardware on Lewis," - an old time hardware store and a competitor. I was very impressed.

He could have said, "Oh, I think were out of them", or "Try something else", but he didn't. It took less than five minutes, and where do you think I always go first to look for my hardware needs? If something does not fit or feel right for you or the time constraint is too difficult, do everyone a favor and JUST SAY NO!

THE HEART OF THE MATTER

OK, here it is. I tried not to, but I cannot write or speak about customer service or service at all without spouting The Golden Rule: Do unto others as you would have them do unto you. This is it in life and business. Customers will respond to you in the same manner in which you treat them. When you care for your customers and treat them with respect, they will do the same for you. There is no way to get around it. We all know how we like to be treated, and we are shocked and pleased when those who serve us actually do it.

Late one night my wife and I were looking for a place to get dinner. We saw a Grandy's Chicken sign and decided what the heck. We don't usually eat fried chicken, and Grandy's is not even on the list when we do, but it was convenient. We looked at the menu posted and it listed chicken fried steak and country fried steak. My wife likes that kind of stuff, so she asked what the difference was. The young man behind the register took the time to carefully explain the way each was prepared. She selected one and I placed my order. He said that those steaks sitting under the lights had been there a while and that he would cook her a fresh one. It would take six minutes. He said with a smile that he would buy us our drinks because of the wait. I commented that he really knew how to please his customers. He replied, "usually all most of them need is a little bit of conversation." He knew how to serve customers. We now have a good feeling about Grandy's, even though I don't remember anything about the food.

His caring manner and his thoughtful attitude made all the difference in the world. Free Cokes cost very little, and the conversation cost nothing but it made a big impression.

Showing concern for others and their needs must be emphasized to each person in your organization. The goal is not to get and keep customers to build your business, but rather to provide benefit to your customers so that they will build your business.

THANKS A LOT

Showing your appreciation, saying Thank You is great and should be done, but the most powerful tool is a personal Thank You.

We needed a bigger car to haul our growing children. We decided to get rid of our 1987 Honda Accord and buy a minivan. Our Honda was in pretty good shape despite the fact that it had 138,000 miles on it and my wife had had the oil changed at least twice. We took it to get it checked out at Lazar auto repair before we put it up for sell. When we picked it up that afternoon they told us it was in great condition and that they had replaced some missing bolts and made a couple of minor adjustments. They charged us the minimum labor fee, gave us our keys and we left feeling pretty good.

A few days later we received a hand-addressed envelope in the mail. Imagine my surprise to find a Thank You card from Lazar auto repair. Was I ever impressed! Now whenever anyone needs auto repair, where do you think I tell them to go?

Personal mail is one of the easiest and rarest things on Earth these days. When was the last time you received a thank you or even a personal letter? You probably can remember because it was so unusual. Thank You cards are so easy to write and are one of the best tools for keeping customers, I guarantee it.

BE EASY!

Many businesses have set themselves up so that it is very difficult for the employee to provide good customer service. They have established policies and procedures or made unsupported statements that the employee cannot live up to. These companies are hurting themselves by basing their business on something other than customer service.

There is a large dairy store with locations throughout the state that has done just that. They got the bright idea that to compete they needed a drive-up window. Now when I think of a drive-up window service, I think "fast." Well, if you want to dispel that idea quickly, drive up to any Braums Ice Cream Store and order a cone. You will sit there for what seems like an eternity, knowing full well that they must be churning the scoop just for you, and if you want a real test of patience, order something like a milk shake or a hamburger.

They have set themselves up for customer service failure. It has not only affected the speed of service at the window but throughout the operation. Now even the walk-in service has taken a nose-dive.

When I asked them about this, they spouted some excuse that they are not meant to be fast since they make everything to order. I can appreciate that, but how long can it take to dip a blob of ice cream, or throw a piece of dry meat on a bun?

Not only do they have the point of service problem,

but they of course have one of those signs posted on their drive-up window with their pledge of fine service and an 800 number to call if you have a problem. I have called that 800 number several times, once while sitting in the long line waiting for service. The only problem is that when you do get hold of a customer service representative, he or she treats you worse than the person at the window! Another failure in their system which doesn't make me feel any better about them.

To prevent this kind of system error, survey your business, use mystery shoppers, read the complaint cards or listen to the calls that come in. But that is not enough, you must take action upon those requests to truly provide quality service.

"I AM SORRY"

The final key to customer service is to say you are sorry and ask for forgiveness. When you do have times of customer service failure, when you err, do not hide, do not make excuses, do not blame, just say, I am sorry, and how can I make it right? This is the true test of your customer service commitment.

My landscape maintenance business included several large condominium complexes. Acres and acres of turfgrass to be maintained. One morning I got a frantic call from the property manager of one of our larger complexes. I promptly rushed over to see what the problem was. When I arrived, the manager was very upset and pointed out a small area where one of the mowers had cut too low scalping the lawn. I looked at the spot in question and then at the 23 acres of neatly mowed and trimmed lawn and I didn't get it. What did she want me to do? Was she blind? What about the 99.9% we had done perfectly? I tried to point all this out to her, but she would not listen. Needless to say, I was frustrated, hurt, defensive, and thought this person was a stupid idiot. I wasn't going to back down. This situation and my reaction to her complaint left both of us at odds. We did not get our contract renewed and lost a big chunk of our business because we handled several properties for this management company.

I have thought about that a lot since then, and realized that she didn't really care that much about that small strip of grass and probably knew that I couldn't do anything about it. All she really wanted was for me to say, "I'm sorry and that we will try to do better next time."

Most people want you to succeed and are more than willing to forgive you if you take responsibility. We are taught to be proud and to stand up for ourselves, but we often need to swallow our pride and take responsibility for the situation no matter how small it may seem or even whose fault it is.

I have found than nothing will cool a hostile customer

quicker and avoid a nasty scene than a sincere apology and the desire to make it right. I guarantee that you will get more mileage out of this than even good service from the beginning. So don't be afraid to say I'm sorry quickly and often, and then move to making it right.

The attitude of customer service must percolate from the top of the organization and be felt by everyone who comes in contact with it. I know that there are struggles of not enough time, not enough good people, not enough money, but your customers don't know that. They just want you to care about them with a pleasant good day, a friendly smile, a moment to bend your ear, a concern for their needs and an appreciation for them spending their money with you. Plant these principles deep within your people and your business cannot help but grow.

VIC OSTEEN

Vic Osteen has shared information on how to juggle the challenges of life without dropping the ball with audiences ranging from prisoners to presidents, speaking to associations and business audiences across the country.

Vic is a speaker, educator, author, horticulturist and entrepreneur. He has thrown newspapers, slung pizza, owned a plant store in the 70's, established 2 landscape companies and a lawn mower businesses. He has sold cow manure, sprayed lawns and is the director of marketing for Win Seminars.

He taught in the Oklahoma State Prison System for six years and has taught college and high school courses in management and marketing, as well as, a program Landscape and Golf Course Management. Vic has appeared on the NBC Television affiliate, as "Mr. Green Thumb", and a weekly radio call in program.

Vic holds a Degree in Horticulture-Floriculture / Retail Business, a Masters Degree in Trade and Industrial Education and is a Doctoral Candidate in Human Resource Development.

Through Growth Seminars his purpose is to teach people how to enjoy more productive professional and personal lives. His entertaining presentations with a natural perspective provide solutions for better management, employee relations and personal development.

Programs Include:

The Design for Success
The steps to developing a life or business that will insure growth and happiness.

Tools for Teamwork - Growing a better workforce
Methods to turn your workforce into a motivated well oiled machine working together to produce a more enjoyable effective business..

A Legacy of Leadership -The Eleven Step Program to Excellence
How to develop leadership qualities in yourself and others.

Customer Service From The Ground Up
Methods that will help you grow your business through an attitude of service.

Juggling Your Time and Your Life
How to find all the time you will ever need and make every day count.

OTHER PRODUCTS

Everything I Needed to Know I Learned in My Garden - *book* $7.95
161 lessons on life, relationship, and laughter learned from Mother Nature

Seeds of Hope - *quote book* $10.00
Quotes, poems, and thoughts of hope, success and happiness

Leaves of Leadership - *quote book* $10.00
Quotes to help you develop your own leadership style.

The E's of Successful Daily Living-*perpetual calendar* $10.00
31 E words, thought and quotes to keep you going through the year

The Design for Success - *Audio* $10.00
The plan for developing and living a life that you can love.

Only The Best On Leadership - *book* $11.95
The best ideas on developing leadership in yourself and others from many of the same authors in this book.

Developing an Employee Manual - *workbook* $35.00
Produce your own employee manual with instructions, examples and work pages to help you produce a better business.

Timely Thoughts & Techniques -*62, 8.5 x 11 posters* $10.95
Colorful posters to keep you and others motivated and on target.

"Growth is the Key to Success, Plant the Planet" *T-shirt* $20.00
Cool 2 color T-Shirt with graphic to tell the world what you believe.

Please include $5.00 for shipping and handling
Mastercard and Visa Welcome.
For information on Vic's keynotes and seminars, please contact:

Growth Seminars
P.O. Box 52465
Tulsa, Oklahoma, 74152-0465
918/742-8454 • 800/746-8454 • Fax 918/747-3185

7

Only The BEST

ALL BUSINESS IS SHOW BUSINESS! MAKING CUSTOMER SERVICE FUN

BY

SCOTT MCKAIN

CUSTOMER SERVICE

ALL BUSINESS IS SHOW BUSINESS!
MAKING CUSTOMER SERVICE FUN

SCOTT McKAIN, CSP, CPAE

Overnight delivery and cable television, fax machines and video conferencing, interactive training and the Internet. Messages of all types not only surround us, they bombard us.

The challenge for any business is no longer getting a message out...it is getting it <u>through!</u>

Yet, the challenge is significantly more than customer service — and certainly more than mere "attention getting." It is also moving the customers to action — obtaining their loyalty in a time where customer devotion is seldom found.

The benchmark has been raised. A quality product or service is not enough to grab the customer's attention. "Quality" and "Service" have now become the expectations. They are taken for granted. The customer that a business must serve today is different — they <u>demand</u> to be entertained, knocked-out and astounded — or, they will look somewhere else.

Consider this point: In the United States alone, at least one million new businesses a year are being created. The competition — and the clutter — is growing dramatically. How does a business make its customer service stand out?

In my speeches, articles and seminars, I always take the unique position that there is a new commandment in American business: **"Thou shalt <u>entertain</u> thy customer while providing quality products and exceptional service."**

No industry is better able to grab our attention and motivate us to action than the entertainment industry. The unique genius they possess is in their ability to capture our consciousness in a manner unlike any other segment of business.

Because of my background in both business and entertainment, I have developed the concept that *all businesses need to apply the attention-getting techniques of show business.*

If you do not know how to excite your customer — no matter what your product is — you are dead in the water with today's consumer.

Make it fun

The essential element in making your customer service different and better is found in making your service fun. It should be fun for the customer and the employee. And, yes, the proper word is FUN!

When stating this concept at a recent workshop I was conducting, the CEO of the billion dollar company to whom I was speaking asked, "Scott, by this do you mean that at some point during the transaction the customer should attain a modicum of enjoyment?"

For once, I was briefly speechless! "No," I finally exclaimed! "I mean it has to be FUN! And, if a 'modicum of enjoyment' is what you are providing, you aren't doing nearly enough!"

According to a study just released by the America's Research Group, **70% of customers** who have experienced entertainment in a business want to return for another visit. About 40% of customers in the same study strongly indicated they would like to see MORE entertainment ideas added to the business environment.

Britt Beemer, chairman of the research firm that prepared the study, said, "Consumers keep saying they have less time to shop, and our research shows that they are indeed shopping less because they are working more hours. So, it makes sense to find better ways to make the business experience more enjoyable in order to encourage shoppers not only to enter the store but also to remain longer, and to come back again," he pointed out. Businesses are now asking whether entertainment will help move them ahead of their competitors. According to the results of this study, Beemer reported that, <u>"The answer is yes."</u>

In his recent "Trend Letter" of September 14, 1995, John Naisbitt wrote that if you "want to sell, teach, inform? First, **entertain**. Entertainment plays an increasingly vital role in our lives. Qualities of fun and amusement once associated mainly with leisure activities are now <u>expected</u> from serious aspects of life, as well. Throughout society, *the underlying strategy in managing, marketing and informing is shifting from boring to entertaining."*

If you agree with Naisbitt — and he has certainly proved to be on-target with many of his predictions of trends — the question MUST become, "How do we do it? How do we make our service experience FUN?"

The New Formula

I believe there is a new formula in how business is conducted.

Here is what is currently happening in today's marketplace:

Sameness (between your product and that of your competition) + **Sameness** (between how you sell and the style of your competitor) + **Sameness** (in the service you provide and how you treat the customer compared to the service of your competition) = **Boredom + Apathy + Commodity Pricing.**

In other words, if there is little differentiation between

you and your competition in the areas of service, product and selling styles, the customer becomes bored, apathetic and price conscious. The important point it that it does not matter if the sameness is real or not. If it perceived by the customer the result is the same, whether it is true or not.

However, it is possible to change the playing field with a new formula. In my speeches and workshops on my topic, "All Business is Show Business™," I introduce this change strategy:

Differentiation (product) + **Entertainment** (customer experience) + **Creativity** (sales and service) = **Excitement + Loyalty + A Focus Upon <u>You</u> and Not Your Price!**

When you differentiate your product in some manner or another; when you become creative in the kind of experience that the customer has with you; and, when you excel in making it fun for all involved, customers become excited, loyal and focus upon you more than the charge for your goods or services.

You may be saying, "Wait a minute. My company builds widgets and there's not much new in widget making. How do we make it different?"

Remember this show business example: The plot of "Star Wars" is at least as old as the movie serials of the 1930's and 40's. However, it was the creativity and storytelling genius of George Lucas that turned the old plot into something special. It has also saturated the national culture and made well over a billion dollars.

"Twenty Master Plots" is one of the best selling books in the writer's market. The author, Ronald B. Tobias, suggests that of all the plays ever produced, movies ever made and shows ever seen there are only twenty plots. It is the creativity of the artist that makes the difference between "High Noon" and "Heaven's Gate."

How creative are you? If this not your area of expertise, hire a consultant! Find a way to take off the blinders and see your business in a new light. Choose friends to by "mystery shoppers" and then report to you on the experience your company provides. Just remember that it has to be FUN! (And, if it is not, you are in trouble!)

The Customer is Different

The main reason that service must become fun is because today's customer is different!

If you were still serving the customer of yesterday, you could still use the same method. It seems a little trite to say you cannot play the game of basketball by using the rules of hockey. Yet, that is exactly what many businesses are trying to do in today's world of customer service. They are trying to serve today's customer using the rules of a game that is not being played.

The loyal customer of yesterday has been replaced by the quick-decision, zap-your-business consumer. Studies in the banking industry, for example, have shown that your parents probably had their checking and savings accounts, car loan and mortgage all at the same bank. My guess is that you will find your own experience to be dramatically different!

Why are we no longer loyal to banks and other businesses? Because we are <u>different</u> from the customers of a few years ago. Most businesses, however, are still trying to treat us as they did our parents — maybe even our grandparents!

For instance, my research with the real estate business clearly shows that people buy a house differently than in the past. My wife and I are currently in the process of buying a new house. It has become obvious that our needs — a quick transaction, making the move to the new location easy, taking possession of the house at a time I am not on the road and others — are not the needs that our current real estate agent is used to handling. He is accustomed to interest rates, price range, number of bedroom and size of the yard.

While money is certainly important to us, we are willing to give a little bit to get the convenience we seek. The house is a big purchase, so we want to get in the house and do painting and re-carpet before we move our belongings. We are finding, however, blank looks from real estate agents when we tell them that this is of vital interest to us. For some agents, if you cannot fit into <u>their</u> perception of what the customer is supposed to be, then you are not a "serious" buyer.

The way in which many real estate agents "show" the properties have not changed to meet the times. Today's buyer is pretty smart. We do not need tour guides. If I hear one more agent take my wife and me into a room with a refrigerator, oven and microwave, and announce, "And, this is the **kitchen!!!**", I am going to scream!

In another example, many car salesmen use sexist terminology, ignoring the fact that most purchasers of automobiles are female! That is not smart, it is clearly wrong — and, it makes no business sense!

Does your business have staffing problems? How about delivery challenges? Anything else bothering you or your business? Please remember this — *the customer of today does not care!*

Most of us are busy, and have little time to transact any kind of business — personal or professional! We are under such stress and time constraints, that if you or your business is having a problem, if you cannot make the transaction quick and fun and the service outstanding, then we will simply go someplace else. Your problems are **your** problems: They are *not the customer's problems.*

Customers of today are kind of like inverse-Amish. There are no barn-raisings for the greater good — we are busting our tails just to get our own stuff done. And, the brighter and more appealing you can make anything, the greater the likelihood we will be attracted to it.

Know Your Customer to Serve Them

It is a very basic question: If you do not know your customer, how will you ever serve them?

But, here is another question that may prove more difficult: How many of the professionals employed by your business are actually members of your "audience"? In other words, **do you hire the people who actually use your product and/or service?**

There are many benefits to be gained when you have that kind of input in a business. Here are two examples:

- Laundry detergent is always trying to be "whiter and brighter." My research into "knowing your customer" uncovered an example that is very revealing. What the <u>customers</u> of laundry soap really wanted was a **package** that was easier to use, store and carry. Detergents that have re-packaged to meet their customer needs have increased sales. The reason for the error in this example was because the people making the decision were "detergent-people" — not "customer-people."

- According to government reports, about one-third of the population of the United States is considered "overweight." And, while it is difficult to think of anything more fattening than potato chips and Frito's, by 1998

one-third of all products from Frito-Lay will be classi-
fied as "low fat." You cannot custom-design your product for your customer from your perspective. It **must**
be from the customer's perspective!

One of the real keys to this show business approach is
that your audience can spot instantly whether or not you
really know them. If you make laundry soap, hire a home-
maker! If you make school buses, hire someone who drives
them every day on country roads! If you make movies,
hire people who represent the audience the movie is trying to reach!

You will be amazed at what you learn.

To differentiate yourself from the rest of the marketplace, make certain your customer service is fun; that you
know your customer of today is different from the one of
the past; and, know your customer inside and out — and
design your service to meet their needs!

Enjoy yourself as you tackle these challenges. After
all, there is "no business like show business." And, ALL
business is show business!

SCOTT MCKAIN

As a professional speaker, seminar leader, and consultant, Scott McKain has received rave reviews over the past 15 years. With topics ranging from customer service and communication, achievement and motivation, Scott can tailor his programs to any audience with a blend of cutting-edge information and  sharp humor. He provides solid information in an entertaining package–a winning combination for any audience.

Scott has given presentations for audiences which range in size from 20 to 10,000+, for international companies, state organizations, and non-profits. He has satisfied each one by working with them to customize his presentation to their specific needs, adding a touch of wit to send the message home.

Scott grew up in rural America, and brings his knowledge of "real people" to each presentation he makes. His leadership skills developed early–he was elected a National Officer of FFA, an organization of over half a million members, before graduating from college. Other honors include being on several presidential committees, being named in "Who's Who in the Midwest" and a Jaycees "Outstanding Young Men in America." In addition to his speaking career, Scott also has a successful commentary show syndicated to over 80 stations across the US, Canada, and Australia.

OTHER PRODUCTS

Just Say YES! A Step Up To Success! • *The seven cassette, fourteen day program to personal achievement that started it all! As seen on national TV!!! Learn the importance of values and priorities, goal setting and communication, and the "Six Steps Up To Success!" Sold on national television for $79.95 . . . special price for Only The Best readers:* $49.95

Just Say YES! A Step up To Success • *The hot-selling book based on the audio cassette album. With a foreword by baseball hall of famer, Jim Palmer! A must read!!! In bookstores for $29.95 . . . special Only The Best price:* $19.95

Just Say YES! A Step Up To Success! • *A full-hour video of the best of the entertainment and enlightenment of Scott McKain.*
(VHS format only) $19.95

Dragonslayers! • *Scott's first audio program. Recorded live and in-studio. The cassettes of humor and information on change, humor and relationships. (Limited quantities available.)* $19.95

Single audio tape of fun with Scott! *Laugh and learn. some of the best of Scott's classic humor and some new fun with a master of message and merriment!* $10.00

SAVE!!! get the whole package for only $99.95

Visa, Master Card, and American Express accepted.
Please include $4.50 for shipping and handling.

For more information contact:
McKain Performance Group
P. O. Box 24800
Indianapolis, IN 46224
800-297-5844
317-875-0708
FAX 317-875-0038

8

Only The **BEST**

THE SERVICE BASICS THAT CREATE CUSTOMER LOYALTY

BY

LISA FORD

CUSTOMER SERVICE

THE SERVICE BASICS THAT CREATE CUSTOMER LOYALTY

Lisa Ford

If your company is like most, you have more competitors than ever before and many of them have the same products, services, prices and promotions. As your products and services become more of a commodity, you must deliver service that differentiates your business. Customers are definitely more savvy, sophisticated and educated. And with their more discerning eye, they must have a reason to do business with you. The single best way to set yourself apart is through high quality distinctive customer service. Customer service that is personalized and customized will keep your customers coming back . Here are the four customer service basics required to create customer loyalty.

Create the total service experience

What is the total service experience? It's the total of every contact the customer has with you and your organization. It is made up of the good times and the bad times, the successes and the failures. Traditionally, customer service has been defined as:

Meet the customer's expectations
Be competent
Respond

Simply satisfying the customer isn't good enough any more. Today the whole concept of customer service has changed from one of satisfying customers to one of *exceeding* their expectations. It takes more than mere competence to win over customers. What customers respond to now is connection, a feeling of making a real bond.

Customers want a partnership with your organization. A partnership is defined as when the customer feels you are on their side working to provide solutions for their specific situation. Partnerships create loyalty and make it tough for customers to take their business elsewhere.

Too often service delivery is lackluster and does nothing to build an ally. Customers have always hated waiting in line, being put on endless hold or being given the bureaucratic runaround. While yesterday's customers dislike these practices, today's customers won't put up with them. Instead, they go to another business where they can be helped quickly. That's why more and more service professionals are being trained and empowered to act immediately and decisively on the customer's behalf. Exceptional customer service is:

> Exceed expectations
> Be connected
> Respond now

When a customer deals with your organization, she has a set of expectations. After she deals with you, she forms a perception. Exceptional customer service equals perception minus expectations.

Where do expectations come from? Here are a variety of sources:

- Advertising
- Previous experience with your product, service or organization
- Reputation
- Competitors' service - "If they can do it, why can't you?"

What do customers want?

1. Customers want you to listen. This shows respect and concern.
2. Customers want you to take responsibility. Walk them through the problem and to a solution.
3. Customers want you to pay attention to the details.
4. Customers want you to remember it is their time and money. You're not doing them a favor. They're doing you one.

When customers don't get what they want, they leave. Customer loss is expensive. It costs five times as much to attract a new customer as it does to keep a customer you currently serve. Exceptional service professionals stay exceptional by seeking feedback. Here are two rules winners follow:

1. They beg for complaints. Finding out what the customer thinks will make things even better. Analyze the information and make the appropriate changes and improvements.

2. They are responsive. On-the-spot resolution is best. Follow the iron law of customer feedback: Respond in 24 to 48 hours. Even if you don't have a complete answer, let the customer know that progress is being made.

Research shows that if the customer feels you are responsive to a problem, he will do business with you again in 82 percent to 95 percent of the cases. In fact, loyalty to your company will actually increase because you were so responsive.

A lost customer is never just one sale or even just one customer. Research shows a satisfied customer will tell four to five other people. When you have a dissatisfied customer, she tells nine to 12 others, possibly building on the story each time.

Deliver service with heart

Customers have basic needs other than completing a simple business transaction. They want to feel welcome, important, valued and understood. And there's no better or easier way to show your customers respect, concern and understanding than really listening to them.

Everyone knows listening is a valuable skill, yet it is not practiced often. There's an old saying, "There is a difference between listening and waiting for your turn to talk." Most people spend their time waiting for their turn to talk. Active listening is a real skill.

Hearing is just processing sounds. When you actively listen, you seek the meaning of the words and the unspoken messages behind them. In addition to facts, you evaluate the tone, emotion and context of the situation. The goal is not just to listen, but to understand the other person. And then to let her know you understood. The five steps of active listening are:

1. Be ready to listen. Have paper and pencil handy, and have your computer cleared and ready for the next contact.

2. Be ready to take notes. If you are on the phone, let the customer know you are taking notes with phrases such as "I'm concerned about this. I'm writing it down."

3. Show you are listening. Use your body language, stance, posture and eye contact. Try phrases such as "I see" to let the customer know you are listening.

4. Ask questions. Get the customer to talk and find out what she really wants.

5. Restate the situation. Don't just repeat. Rephrase the customer's statements by putting the message in your own words. Don't restate the entire idea, just the main points. Restating also invites corrections from the customer so you'll know you're on the right course.

Listening is an important skill that connects you with the customer. Here are other skills that help you deliver service with heart and professionalism:

Build rapport with your customers. To provide service with heart and make that all-important emotional connection with the customer, use these four critical strategies.

1. Use the customer's name. Say the customer's full name and title, such as Ms. Smith or Dr. Jones. If the customer wants to be less formal and on a first-name basis, follow his lead. British Airways asked their employees to use customers' names when checking boarding passes, tickets and luggage for three months. In that period, customer surveys showed a 60 percent increase in satisfaction.

2. Avoid jargon. If it isn't common knowledge or you wouldn't use these words in everyday conversation with people outside your organization, don't use them with the customer.

3. Be friendly. Give the service you would want to receive. Do it sincerely.

4. Be confident and competent. The customer will want to deal with you.

Sharpen your phone skills. Some times you may have to transfer a customer to better serve him. To keep from feeling like he's getting the runaround, keep him informed and let him know you're not just passing the buck. When you have to transfer a call, remember these tactics:

State what you can do, not what you can't. For example, if the team in accounts payable can handle the call better and give the customer greater satisfaction faster, then you really are helping the customer by transferring her. Don't say, "I can't help you. Let me transfer you." Say, " I can help you by letting you talk to Susan in accounts payable. Let me connect you." This statement is "can" instead of "can't" and the customer will feel cared for and confident that an answer is coming.

Avoid the word "transfer." Try "Let me connect you" or I'll put you in touch with." These words communicate the benefits of your actions clearly to the customer.

Pass along customer information. At the very least, know the customer's name and pass it along to the next employee.

Stay on the line, introduce him to the next employee if possible. That makes the transition easier. Never transfer the call if the other employee isn't available. Connecting him to an endlessly ringing phone will undo all your good actions.

One of the best ways to deliver exceptional customer service is to honor the "one voice concept." Your customer will be more satisfied if he only has to deal with one person instead of being bounced around.

If customers don't like being transferred, they certainly don't like being put on hold. By pushing your hold button a little too quickly or too often, you can easily damage relationships with your customers. The best solution is to not put the customer on hold. You may want to say, "May I have a number where I can reach you? I'll call you back in 10 minutes and I'll have that information for you." After 10 minutes, whether you have that information or not, call the customer. Here are four steps to follow when you must put a customer call on hold:

1. Ask "Are you able to hold?" Wait for her response.

2. Get back to the customer after no more than 45 sec-

onds. Shoot for a maximum of 30 seconds and never go beyond 45 seconds without coming back on the line for an update.

3. Thank you customer for calling. Always say, "Thanks for holding." Avoid saying "I'm sorry you had to hold."

4. Offer to call back instead of putting her on hold. If you know the process is going to take a little extra time, offer to call the customer back at a specific time.

Perfecting your phone skills will make a big difference in the impression you create for the customer.

Please challenging customers

Studies show that only one out of 25 unhappy customers complains. So when you get a customer who's upset, realize there are 24 others who feel the same way but didn't bother to tell you — probably because they felt it wouldn't do any good and quietly took their business some place else. A satisfied customer will be your organization's biggest advocate and more effective than any advertising or marketing campaign.

When customers are emotional, they become difficult, frustrated and quick to anger. And angry customers don't respond to logic. The more logical you are, the angrier it will make them. Here are steps to calm the challenging customer:

1. Stay calm yourself. Take deep breaths to keep your voice open and sound relaxed. When your voice closes, it will sound rushed and panicked, and the customer will hear it.

2. Let the customer vent. Actively listen and let the customer know you're listening through body language. Don't interrupt the customer because she'll just start at the beginning again.

3. Deal with emotions first. A customer can't think logically until you deal with her emotions. Acknowledging the customer's emotions makes her feel valued and helps you develop a partnership with her. Restate the information so the customer knows you listened.

4. Avoid emotional trigger phrases.

Trigger Phrases	Calming phrases
Policy	Here's what we can do
Can't	Can
Sorry	Thank you
No. I don't know	I can find out
Why didn't you	I can see why

When you're dealing with angry or challenging customers, your ultimate goal is to arrive at a solution to the customer's problem. Here are some keys:

- Involve the customer in the solution. Ask him to recommend a solution or say "What can I do to make this right?" If his request is reasonable, grant it. If not, offer a compromise and act quickly on the solution. When a customer is involved in solving the problem, his solution if often less than you were going to offer. And because he thought of it, he'll be more satisfied with the outcome.

- Provide a solution and something extra when you or the organization has been at fault. Customers want things done right the first time and when that doesn't happen, the customer feels hassled. He has to take his time, energy and sometimes money to deal with you the second time. To recover from a service failure you must give the customer something extra; this will lessen the hassle factor. The "something extra" at your company might include free shipping or additional product. For example, a temporary help agency who sends out an employee for a job who did not meet the customer's expectations will not charge for that employee and follows up with a bouquet of flowers with a bottle of aspirin attached. The enclosed card reads, "We are sorry for the headache we caused." That simple gesture creates lots of goodwill and keeps the customer loyal. Great recovery goes a long way.

- Commit to the customer's satisfaction. Give him your name, phone extension and what hours you work so he can contact you directly if he has more questions. If the problem happens again, he has a relationship with you and you know the history of the situation.

Become a service star

As a service professional, you have the opportunity to brighten people's lives, create a positive impression, do a little good, and at the same time achieve some personal satisfaction. Here's what you can do to keep that "can do" attitude going all day long.

1. Listen to your self-talk. Don't clutter your mind with negatives. Eleanor Roosevelt said, "No one can make you feel inferior without your consent." Let your personality shine through.

2. Use a calming object. Post a thank-you note from a customer in your work area. Placing a mirror by your phone will help you see the "smile" in your voice and body language as you talk with a customer on the phone.

3. Focus on successes. Don't play the "ain't it awful" game with co-workers during your lunch time, seeing who has the worst customer story of the day. Instead, focus on how you took one unhappy customer through the process and got a satisfying result.

4. Develop a buddy system. You can learn problem solving strategies from each other.

5. Maintain your sense of humor. Laugh at yourself and laugh with your customers. Take your sense of humor to work and make certain to take it back home.

Your role in dealing with customers is crucial to the continued success of your company. Customers want a partnership with you and your organization. When you deliver exceptional service, customers will return. Remember customer loyalty is earned one transaction at a time. You are only as good as your last move. Provide your customers with the total service experience as you consistently exceed their expectations and you will have a customer for life.

LISA FORD

**Author Of The
#1 Selling Business
Videotape Series
*"How To Give
Exceptional
Customer Service"***

Lisa Ford delivers what her audiences want - practical ideas combined with plenty of opportunities to laugh and relate to her examples. Her content inspires people to increase their personal, team and organization's results.

Lisa is the author of *How To Give Exceptional Customer Service*, the #1selling business videotape series for the last 3 years in the U.S. She has also authored, *Developing A Customer Retention Program*, co-authored *Building A Customer Driven Organization: The Manager's Role* video and audio tapes, and *Personal Power* audiotapes. She specializes in the field of customer service, customer retention, managing, hiring and training for service excellence. Other popular topics offered by Lisa are on leadership, management, everyday excellence and communications.

Lisa's experience includes working with many of the nation's best: SmithKline Beecham, Equitable, Viacom, CSX and Georgia Power. She presents over 100 speeches and seminars yearly across the United States, United Kingdom and Australia.

Over the years, Lisa has customized numerous videos for clients to use in their ongoing training efforts. She is highly rated and a favorite speaker at the International Customer Service Association where she speaks annually.

Audiences love Lisa's energy, enthusiasm, humor, practical techniques and common sense messages. After her presentations, organizations love the change in attitudes, increased awareness and improved results.

Lisa's Programs Include

- *Why Customer Service Is Not Enough*
  - Focus On Satisfaction, Loyalty and Retention
  - Exceed Expectations As A Daily Discipline

- *Everyday Excellence*
  - Create And Add Value To Increase Your Results
  - Maintain An Attitude Of Enthusiasm

- *How To Lead And Manage In Today's Crazy Workplace*
  - Understand The Role Of The New Manager
  - Love And Master Change

OTHER PRODUCTS

How To Give Exceptional Customer Service $299.95
The Nation's best selling video series. 4 volumes plus workbook covering how to make each contact memorable and keep customers satisfied. Great for training sessions.

How To Give Exceptional Customer Service $79.95
4 audio tape program, great for anyone who has contact with customers. Terrific how-to's, stories and examples.

Developing a Customer Retention Program $59.95
4 audio tapes on how to increase repeat business and build loyalty. Lots of action ideas.

Inspiring Everyday Excellence $10.00
An audio tape recorded live, covering personal excellence, service excellence and leadership excellence. Very motivational.

Six Ways To Be A Service Leader $10.00
An audio tape recorded live, with action steps to exceed customer's expectations and lead to inspire great service. Includes Lisa's memorable dry cleaners story.

Please add $4.00 Shipping & Handling

For more information contact:
Ford Group, Inc.
140 Seville Chase
Atlanta, Georgia 30328
770-394-4860 • FAX 770-394-0034

9

Only The BEST

Six Key Steps To Hiring For Customer Service

By

Mel Kleiman

CUSTOMER SERVICE

Six Key Steps To Hiring For Customer Service

Mel Kleiman

In today's quest for organizational excellence, the key to a successful organization is **its people**. The business world is competitive, yet all businesses have the same access to available resources. The one true asset you have that separates you from your competition is the ability to select the people who work for you.

People make the difference. Your employees are the ones who make the sales, make the customers happy, and make the customers want to come back. They are also the ones who can lose the sales, upset the customers, and make the customers stay away.

As determined in the rest of this book, more businesses lose customers because of the attitude of an employee toward the customer than for any other reason. **It is much easier to *hire* a customer service attitude than to *train* one.** Therefore, it is important to determine the basic customer service attitudes of all applicants before you consider hiring them to deal with your customers.

1. IDENTIFY WHAT YOU NEED

In order to successfully hire the right person for a customer service job, you must identify what you are looking for in an employee, and the key attributes that would make this employee successful on the job. In other words, you can't hit the target unless you know what the target looks like. This is also similar to putting together a jigsaw puzzle. If you don't look at the picture on the front of the box to see what the puzzle is supposed to look like when it's finished, it is ten times more difficult to know where the pieces belong.

The most effective way to identify what traits are needed to do the job well is to analyze the job, focusing on what needs to be accomplished in that position. You must define the objectives of the job, as well as the responsibilities of the job holder. Compose a written job analysis, rather than just a job description. A job analysis directly reflects the job today, as well as its potential for the future, similar to a motion picture. A job description is merely a static instrument that describes the job as it was, more like a snapshot.

The following questions should be carefully considered when composing a job analysis:
- Why does this job exist?
- What are the main responsibilities of the job?
- What must this person do well to earn a raise?

- Why would you reprimand or fire this person?
- What did the last jobholder do well? Do not so well?

The key competencies of a customer service employee generally fall into four primary categories:

1. **Capacity** - What proficiencies are required to do the job? Is this person both mentally and physically capable of performing the job?
2. **Attitude** - What dispositions are needed for success in this job? Is the applicant honest? Dependable? Safe? Customer Oriented?
3. **Personality** - What temperament is needed to fit into your organizational environment? Is the candidate a team player? Enthusiastic? Friendly?
4. **Skills** - What expertise is required to do the job? Does this person have the skills necessary to handle the job, or to be easily trained?

2. A MARKETING APPROACH TO RECRUITING

Once you have "painted the picture on the box" and know what type of person you are looking for, you are ready for applicants. Unfortunately, the good ones usually don't walk up to you and ask for a job. Just as you would actively recruit to find good customers, you must actively recruit to locate good customer service employees.

Recruiting is selling, and you have to sell your organization to the right type of applicant. Focus your recruiting efforts on people who give *you* good customer service.

Some of the most effective ways to recruit good applicants are to internally promote reliable employees, to re-hire past employees, referrals from current employees, referrals from other applicants, and through the newspaper if you advertise effectively.

Since you know from your job analysis the type of applicant you are trying to attract, determine where these people: congregate, socialize and entertain, work, play, belong, shop, live, obtain information, participate in the community, etc. — then go out and find them!

The best possible time to recruit is before you have a job opening to fill. Recruiting is an on-going process — if you wait until you need the person, it's too late! Always be on the lookout for your **next** employee.

3. <u>USE OF HIRING TOOLS AND PRE-EMPLOY-MENT TESTING</u>

The U.S. Government says that everything you do in the hiring process is a test. Even with targeted recruiting, unqualified customer service candidates will appear. You must test applicants during every step of the hiring process to save time, money and reduce your legal exposure.

Telephone screening interviews can be an excellent source of information about a candidate, and give valuable insight into their personality. For example, if you need a customer service representative who will have a lot of phone contact with your customers, you can easily determine the person's phone manner and attitude in just a few moments on the phone. If they are not courteous and friendly to you, they will not be courteous and friendly to your customers. Don't make the mistake of letting a phone screen take the place of an in-depth, face-to-face interview. Some people are very polite and charming on the phone, but quite the opposite in person.

Application blanks are also used to pre-screen applicants before the interview. Tell the applicant to fill out the application completely, leaving no blanks nor referring to a resume. If the applicant does either of these after being instructed not to, dismiss him/her as a candidate based on an unwillingness or inability to follow instructions. After all, what you see in the application and interview process is better than you will ever see again in your entire life.

Computer based or pen and paper evaluations are another vital tool used to identify and measure the customer service attitudes and personality of the applicant. These evaluations can help predict the amount of client interaction that the applicant prefers, and how well he or she will relate to the needs and concerns of your customers. Will the applicant lose his/her cool when dealing with multiple tasks? Will he/she be able to handle rush times and still service everyone with a smile? These are important things to know before you hire someone for customer service.

Studies have found that the key to predicting whether a candidate will be a good employee is their **attitude**, not skills. The U.S. Labor Department says that over 87% of all people fail, not because of capability, but because of personality and attitude. Attitude evaluations can measure the attitudes that are vital to productive, motivated employees, such as dependability, initiative, values, and customer service. **Personality** plays a big part in determining whether or not a person is right for a particular job. Personality traits such as competitiveness, dominance, sociability, subjectivity, self-consciousness, emotional awareness, and more can be measured to help match a person's personality to the job.

Some examples of true/false questions asked on these evaluations dealing with customer service include:
1. I find it easy to talk to people.
2. I find it hard to be nice to people who won't do things my way.
3. The motto, "The customer is always right," is more important today than ever before.
4. I lose my temper easily.
5. I like helping people.
6. When a customer is rude to me, it is okay to put them in their place or ignore them.
7. I work hard to get along with everyone.
8. I like a job with lots of customer contact.

Drug Screening is now used by seventy percent of the Fortune 500 companies as a pre-employment requirement.

If you don't do drug testing and your competition does, the drug users will all want to work for you! Therefore, employment should be contingent on passing a drug screen.

Skills testing, another test in the hiring process, measures an applicant's level of proficiency in certain areas, such as math, typing speed, computer knowledge, intelligence, mechanical ability, etc. Have the applicant perform any skill that will be required on the job.

4. THE INTERVIEW

Once you have determined that the applicant has compatible customer service attitudes, personality, and skills for the job, it is time to move on to the interview. In order to easily compare applicants, you should ask each applicant the same questions. This will provide consistency and lower liability. Interview the applicant in a relaxed setting, and ask open-ended questions that require them to do most of the talking while you listen carefully and observe.

The following are some key questions you should ask every applicant you interview:
1. What made you respond to the ad?
2. What hours and days do you prefer to work? (Caution: if you hire an employee to work shifts they are willing to work, but prefer not to, chances are they will eventually become dissatisfied.)
3. If hired, how long do you plan to stay on the job?

4. Tell me about your very first paying job. How did you get that job? Why did you get it? How long did you work there? What did you learn from it? (These questions show what levels of responsibility were taken and how seriously the applicant took these responsibilities.)
5. Tell me about the job you enjoyed the most, the least, and why?
6. What do you feel it takes to be good at customer service?
7. What is the most difficult customer service problem you have ever encountered, and how did you handle it?
8. Why should I hire you and why shouldn't I hire you?
9. What else would you like to tell me about yourself?

Pay close attention to the answers and *how* they are given. Remember, what you see in the interview process is better than you will ever see again. If they don't smile in the interview, they will probably not smile much on the job. Hint: It is much easier to **hire** a friendly person than to **train** a person to be friendly!

5. <u>GETTING REFERENCES AND VERIFICATION</u>

Next, you need to confirm that what you see is what you get! The best indicator of an applicant's future performance is his/her past performance, so **check references.**

According to the Society for Human Resource Management, 20% to 25% of all resumes and applications contain *at least* one major discrepancy. Some of the most common include: wrong date of employment, falsification of education/dates/courses/degrees, exaggerated previous experience and salaries, nonexistent former employers, and omission of relevant negative information.

If you hire someone who has falsified their employment record, you can be held accountable and risk a negligent hiring lawsuit. Carefully screening your applicants can help minimize this risk. Make sure to always:

- Verify education and prior employment,
- Thoroughly explore employment gaps during the interview, and
- Get written permission from the applicant to check his/her references, **then do it!**

Checking references can be a challenge, however. Many employers have been sued successfully by former employees claiming that false information regarding their past performance was given. This makes employers hesitant to release information, but having written permission from the applicant can help. If met with resistance when checking references, try one of the following strategies:

1. There have been Reference Verification Forms developed to help gather information. These are successful about 95% of the time, so use one!
2. Ask a different member of your department to try. Sometimes the compatibility developed between the reference checker and the reference can make all the difference.

3. Ask to speak with a former co-worker of the applicant, rather than a supervisor. You may get a willing response from someone else.

4. If nothing else works, appeal to the reference's common sense. Ask how *they* hire new customer service employees without checking references.

5. Develop a positive relationship with the reference if they start to open up. This will often help you get more information. Also, remember to pay attention not only to *what* is said, but *how* it is said!

6. <u>ORIENTATION</u>

Finally, make sure you have an efficient orientation program for your employees. You only have one chance to make a first impression on a new employee, and this will set the tone for the relationship you will have with this employee. An orientation system can either be supportive and helpful to the employee, or will set the employee up for failure and dissatisfaction.

Keep in mind that your employees will probably treat your customers the same way you treat them, so always treat them with courtesy and respect. Everyone should have a job where at least part of what they do interests them, so give employees an opportunity to do what they like to do whenever you can. Encourage them to be informed, ask questions, share information with others, and to be a part of the team. Give your employees the opportunity to perform, learn, and grow on the job. Hint: Happy, satisfied employees work harder, get more accomplished on the job, and give better service to your customers!

MEL KLEIMAN

Mel Kleiman is a professional speaker, consultant, and nationally recognized leading authority in the area of **Employee Recruiting, Selecting, and Hiring.** He is the co-founder and president of Humetrics, Inc., one of the nation's most prominent organizations specializing in the development and implementation of Employee Selection Systems.

To succeed in business today, companies must improve customer service, increase sales, and reduce losses. Mel believes the best way to accomplish this is through the recruiting, selecting, and hiring of competent, motivated, and productive employees.

Mel is a high impact speaker with high impact information on a high impact topic. His dynamic and energetic presentations teach audiences how to hire the right person for the right job on the very first try. Both large companies and small businesses enjoy, learn, and improve their businesses because of his programs and presentations. After attending one of Mel's sessions, you will have obtained useful, "take-home" information tailored to your company's needs that can immediately help you hire people who will help your company prosper and grow.

As a consultant, Mel designs and delivers various types of programs dealing with the selection process. Author of *Blueprint for Successful Hiring*, a "how to" manual on everything from developing job descriptions to making the offer, Mel provides solutions to those tough hiring dilemmas. Mel shares his in-depth knowledge of employee selection as a featured radio and television guest, and through numerous articles in trade journals and publications.

ABOUT HUMETRICS

Humetrics is a nationally recognized boutique consulting firm which provides services and products that help companies recruit and select better employees. Founded in 1976, the company began as a broad-based human resource firm. Over the past ten years we have narrowed our mission to focus specifically on the hiring process.

The staff of Humetrics devotes effort, insight, and creativity in assisting clients in re-engineering their selection system to identify, recruit, and select the best candidates in the marketplace. Over the last ten years we have become a prime resource with regards to the recruiting and selection of employees to hundreds of companies throughout the U.S. We repeatedly accomplish this through:

- Educational Presentations and Workshops
- Internal Consulting Services
- Development of Customized Selection Systems
- State-of-the-Art Proprietary Selection Tools (Software & Hardware)
- Customer Service and Support

We are dedicated to solving the recruiting and selection problems of our clients, surpassing expectations, and continually improving our businesses.

For more information, please contact:
Humetrics, Inc.
8300 Bissonnet, Suite 490
Houston, Texas 77074
phone 713-771-4401 fax 713-771-0501

CUSTOMER SATISFACTION:
THE GAME YOU JUST CAN'T WIN

ROXANNE EMMERICH

CUSTOMER SERVICE

Customer Satisfaction: The Game You Just Can't Win

Roxanne Emmerich

Everything is going well. Your top customer tells you they love you. They give you a 6.9 out of 7 on your customer satisfaction survey. Then it happens. They leave you for a better price offered by your competitor. How could they? The nerve! Don't they know how good you are? What would it take? What more can you do?

If you're still focusing on customer satisfaction, you may not be aware that you're playing the wrong game. Customer satisfaction is important, but despite your great customer service, they will leave you for a better price. Oh, the divorce might be friendly, and they may even court you again, but they're having the affair anyway.

It's easy to get somebody's business. What's challenging is to get the business, keep the business, and maintain your profit margins while you do. So how do you keep your customers without getting into a price war?

Customer satisfaction merely gets you in the game. If you want to keep the business, you need to make sure your customers are <u>successful</u>. If you do that well, they will never leave you. The problem is most organizations are so focused inwardly that they shoot themselves in the foot. This can happen to you when the emphasis is on <u>your</u> bottom line, <u>your</u> sales growth, <u>your</u> customer satisfaction index.

The critical part of the equation that you may be missing is this: Without customers, your business is not successful. Your customers decide whether you get to keep playing the game. Not only do you need customers, you need to keep them for life. They sometimes will leave you even if they're satisfied. But if you help them succeed, they're not going anywhere.

Sounds great in theory but how do you go about helping your customers succeed?

Go beyond their wants to their needs.

Customers rarely understand what they need. Oh, they will tell you what they want, but they often require your help to uncover what they need.

A large part of my consulting practice is dedicated to speaking at corporate and association conferences. When people call our office to hire a speaker for an upcoming meeting, they almost always respond the same way when we ask them how they will judge the success of my program. "The evaluations will be great."

Good evaluations are what they want, but what they need goes much deeper. Good evaluations are important—they show that everyone in the audience was delighted. Customer satisfaction! But, what my customers <u>need</u> is to have their people think differently, feel differently, and most important, they need to do things differently. My job is to uncover what they need to think, feel, and do differently and then help them attain that change of behavior.

I help my customers' success by measurably improving their employees' performance—that of boosting sales, efficiencies, cross-sales, the effectiveness of the executives and therefore that of the employees. A great speech is what they wanted. Better performance is what they <u>need</u>. My job is to focus beyond the goal they set for me to give them what they need. When I help them be more successful, they're not only staying with me for life, but they'll make referrals to everyone they know.

To find in measurable terms what customers need, I ask how they want their people to feel differently. Since feelings drive behaviors, this is the foundation upon which I build everything else. I don't know if it is more shocking or sad that companies spend millions of dollars on teambuilding training without ever talking about the issues that are breaking down trust. These are scary issues and usually it hurts to talk about them, yet doing so has breakthrough potential to unlock creativity, focus, better interdepartmental relationships, and more.

Whether you are selling sausage, computers, bank services, or health care, there is always a way to dramatically improve your customer retention and referrals if you focus on making your customers successful. Here are five areas for you to focus on as you look for opportunities to solidify your relationships with your customers:

- **Find and refer potential customers to them.**

Just as you need referrals, so do your customers. If you don't believe enough in what your customers are doing, then you shouldn't be doing business with them anyway. You want to work with successful vendors and customers. Their income will be reflected directly in your income. If you believe in what they do, think of all the people or businesses that potentially could use their product or service and make the connection. It costs you nothing and will pay back huge rewards.

- **Help them find employees.**

Ask any employer today, and they will tell you that one of their biggest challenges is finding employees who are skilled and possess the right attitudes. When you put an ad in the paper, the majority of the applicants are unemployed. That's not the pool that will produce the best results from the least effort. Because you are in business, your sphere of influence can help you connect your customers with many people who possess the right attitudes and skills for the positions they are attempting to fill.

- **Train your customers' employees.**

Several years ago, a Malcolm Baldridge award winner benchmarked its training efforts and found they received at 30-1 return for each dollar spent on employee training. Since training your people offers your organization tremendous opportunity for improving your bottom line, it is probably safe to assume that the same happens with your customers' employees.

Offer to train them in areas both related to and unrelated to your product. A software company should consider not only training its customers' employees on how to use the software product and how to sell it better, but it may want to show them how to improve their displays at the store. Perhaps the customer's employees could use some general sales training, or maybe they could be coached on their inventory procedures to improve their efficiencies.

Where do you think your customer will bring additional business if you do that? I'll bet they won't even mind a price premium over your competitors who are merely selling their wares.

- **Maintain price integrity.**

While working with a computer software company, the sales manager told me that their main product sold for $80,000. I asked him how often they negotiated the price. "Slightly over 100 percent of the time," he said with a sheepish grin. Actually, they negotiated price in every case.

Negotiating price creates a win-lose scenario. It creates an adversarial relationship. Worse yet, it creates a situation where you can never again be perceived as being on the same side of the fence. Also, once you jump on this bandwagon, it's hard to get off. They always expect it.

It's difficult to haggle on price with a customer and then turn around and say you are there to help them be successful. Not only are you losing your margins, you are losing your rapport. I believe there is only one answer to a price objection: "The price is cast in stone, but everything else is negotiable. How else can we help you get what you need?" This creates a dialogue in which you can find out what they really need. By uncovering those needs and setting a plan to meet them, you have bonded and gained unparalleled respect. They feel they are getting a great value.

Customers will respect you for your pricing and feel comfortable knowing that their competition is not getting a better deal. They will also get more of what they

want or what you uncover that they need. Negotiate anything but price!

- **Keep talking.**

The best way to keep in contact is to call your past
customers occasionally and ask, "How's things?" It may
not be grammatically correct, but it will tremendously
improve your relationship with your customer and will
increase your sales significantly. The magic is in keeping
silent following the question. As they begin to tell you of
their challenges, their wins, what their competition is
doing, etc., notice the opportunities for you to help them.

There is no better question because it allows the customer to take the conversation wherever they want and
share with you things you would never otherwise find out.
Make sure that when you are silent, you are not just con-
centrating on keeping silent. Instead, this is a time to creatively think of ways you can reinforce their wins, improve their margins, and find out about the areas that are
holding them back from performing closer to their potential.

Making the Switch

Making a switch from a customer satisfaction mentality to a customer success mentality requires a whole
different way of leading people. You need to stop asking
only for behavior from your people but instead lead them

with a vision that enlists their hearts, minds, and souls. This is difficult to conceptualize. The best way I know to explain this is to share a story:

As I traveled to Paris on Christmas Day with my buddy Fahden, we were discussing on the plane what we wanted to make happen on that trip. I surprised myself as I began to share with him what I wanted. "You know how in the movies, French men enchant women by delicately kissing a woman's hand while looking passionately into her eyes. That's what I want, Fahden! I want a French man to kiss my hand."

Fahden's only reply was, "No problem, we can make that happen."

On the fifth day of our trip, I said, "Fahden, we only have two days left and my hand still hasn't been kissed. They think we're an item and you're scaring them off." Fahden concurred, "Say no more. Just point out the kind of man you want and he's yours."

As we walked into the next café, I saw a man at the end of the counter. He oozed charm. His eyes were pools of French mystery. He stopped my show! I pointed to him and said, "One like him."

Before I could stop him, Fahden was already whispering to the man with the eyes. And then it happened. His eyes commanded mine. He moved toward me. Time stopped. Without releasing my eyes, he kissed my hand, looked deeply into my eyes and said, "Enchante." I sighed as I thought, "Yes, just like in the movies."

In my most sensuous voice I said, "Hello, my name is Roxanne." He replied (in what sounded more like a New Jersey accent than the alluring French I had imagined), "Hey, I'm Tony. I own the striptease bar down the street. You two want to come?" Whoa, that wasn't in the script, and neither was his smile. As he opened his mouth, all I could see were rotten teeth.

What do kisses and bad teeth have to do with managing the customer success process? It has to do with what we create based on what we ask for. I asked for a kiss on the hand and what I got was rotten teeth. That wasn't exactly the final result I was looking for. Our controlling natures lead us to ask for behaviors: sales calls, quotas, reports, and scripted sales pitches. What we get are sales staff and customer service staff who are stifled. They are doing the job on automatic. The energy and excitement are not there. That's not what we wanted.

What we really want is for our sales and customer service staff to be so excited that their energy draws the customers back to them. We want them to think outside the box to find solutions to improve the success of their customers. We want them to be passionate about their work.

To help our people switch from focusing on customer satisfaction to customer success, we need to change how we lead and manage our organizations. In French terms, we need to stop asking for kisses and instead draw them into a love affair.

Your job in leading outstanding customer success is to enroll your people in a vision of how they can be of service to your customers. Your job is to help them thrive at work and creatively help your customers break through to greater success. You can't get there by controlling people.

For your team to win a football game, it helps to be on the football field instead of on the basketball court. You need to be playing the right game. It's time to leave the customer satisfaction game and get on the field of customer success. The more you help your customers and employees get what they need, the more you will get what you need.

ROXANNE EMMERICH, CSP

Roxanne Emmerich, CSP, is President of The Emmerich Group Inc., a Minneapolis based consulting firm that helps businesses break through to the next level. She is the author of four books including Thank God it's Monday: How to Build a Motivating Workplace and more than 100 articles for various magazines and trade journals.

Successful Meetings magazine has proclaimed Roxanne as one of the top speakers in the country on organizational change. She is the youngest woman business speaker to have received the highest designation of the National Speakers Association, the Certified Speaking Professional, which less than 8% of their membership has attained.

Her reputation for helping organizations improve their productivity earned her an appointment by Governor Tommy Thompson to Wisconsin's highest ranked commission in 28 years. Charged with maximizing the effectiveness of state government, their blueprint for reform is now used as a model for many states and is one of the most widely publicized commission projects ever.

As an executive in charge of starting a new bank and brokerage, she grew deposits form zero to over $35 million in less than two years setting records in growth and profitability. Roxanne co-owned a business that was singled out from over 50,000 others for the top national award in the agri-business industry.

She has coached over one thousand clients including: Northwest Airlines, Dayton Hudson, Monsanto and banks across the country.

For information on speaking or consulting services, contact The Emmerich Group, Inc.

The Emmerich Group, Inc.
One Paramount Plaza
7801 East Bush Lake Road
Suite 360
Minneapolis, MN 55439-3115

1-800-236-5885
e-mail RoxanneEmm@aol.com

OTHER PRODUCTS

Thank God It's Monday: How to Build a Motivating Workplace—Book $6.95
Wouldn't it be great to work in a place you couldn't wait to get to? This book gives you sound and immediately applicable ideas for you to use to improve the excitement, fun and productivity in your workplace.

Dancing With Reckless Abandon—Tape $14.95
Roxanne's most popular keynote address—Includes ideas on how to get people thinking about going beyond their job description to viewing their job as seeing what isn't there and making it happen. Learn how to break through your old work patterns of dancing by number to fully thrive using the formula of: Psyche, Systems and Soul.™

That's Not My Job: How to Make Extraordinary Customer Service Everyone's Focus—Book $6.95
Thirteen ideas to revolutionize your customer service by changing the focus from satisfaction to customer success.

A Workplace to Die For—Video $39.95
You don't have to kill yourself to create a work environment that is "to die for". This televised interview covers easy ways to make your work environment come alive with more excitement, satisfaction and results.

Only the Best on Leadership—Book $11.95
The best ideas on leadership from many of the same authors in this book.
If you liked this book—you'll love *Only the Best on Leadership.*

Want it all? — All 5 items above $60.00

Please include $5.00 shipping and handling.
Mastercard and Visa are welcome.

For information on all Roxanne's books and learning materials, or to book Roxanne to speak at your next meeting or consult with your group, please contact:

The Emmerich Group, Inc.
One Paramount Plaza
7801 East Bush Lake Rd, Suite 360
Minneapolis, MN 55439-3115
1-800-236-5885
e-mail RoxanneEmm@aol.com

CUSTOMER DELIGHT IS EVERYBODY'S BUSINESS

DAN CLARK

CUSTOMER SERVICE

CUSTOMER DELIGHT IS EVERYBODY'S BUSINESS

DAN CLARK

In recent months, I have been the keynote speaker at two national Marriott Hotel conventions. In attendance were their employees and top customers. In preparation for my presentations, I investigated the inside philosophy of Marriott toward its' internal and external customers. Their fundamental principle stood out: It is "Be Brilliant at the Basics."

"The Basics" are fundamental to every success. In music, there are only twelve basic, fundamental notes. And they were discovered way before Beethoven or B.B. King came along. All they did was take these twelve basic notes and arrange them into beautiful, magnificent musical masterpieces. The same holds true in *Customer Service*. By simply being brilliant at the basics, we create that cherished "Wow" experience and turn ordinary expected customer satisfaction into extraordinary unexpected customer "Delight." Let me explain how.

While most are constantly searching for "new" answers, the successful are focusing on the "right" answers. The "right" answers are those certain and specific fundamental principles that have always been, and will always be, the backbone for success. When we stay focused on these fundamentals, we avoid costly cycles of trial and error and vault past our competition with confidence, poise and peak performance.

There are six basic principles and practices necessary to create <u>Customer Delight</u>:

1) **BE BRILLIANT AT HIRING THE RIGHT PERSON.** I realize this sounds trite and appears to be difficult, but it really is easy. When Marriott opened up their huge and elegant Marriott Marquis Hotel in New York City, they interviewed 15,000 people to fill 1,800 employee positions. Consequently, this is one of the finest and best run hotels in the world. What should we look for in hiring the perfect employee? A few years ago, I was at a school for professional baseball scouts. On the program was Mr. George Genovese, one of the most successful baseball scouts of all time. I asked him what he specifically looked for in a potential player. He said he looked for the intangible qualities of success that you cannot teach - work ethic, heart, and desire to win. He also investigated if the young men interacted responsibly in a family setting and if they respected authority. George taught me that when you focus on the intangible qualities of success first, all of the job development skills and productivity prowess will take care of themselves. In other words, when your attitude is right, your abilities will catch up!

2) **BE BRILLIANT AT SETTING TOTAL QUALITY EXPECTATIONS.** When we stretch to set high expectations and then work hard to bring our performance up to meet those high expectations, we call that "*Accomplishment.*" The task was hard. We had to come early and stay late and occasionally go without a break, but it was worth it. It makes us feel good, nurtures healthy self-image, breeds teamwork and inspires total quality performance. In contrast, when we become apathetic and comfortable in our past efforts and settle in on low expectations, and then allow our behavior to slip to meet those low expectations, we call that "*Rationalization.*" Rationalization is killing our corporations. It is easy to rationalize because it is easy to be mediocre. Being a champion and creating customer delight is hard. If it were easy, everybody would do it. The "hard" is what makes it special.

There is a direct correlation between *hiring the right person* and setting quality expectations. One without the other is useless. Let me explain: When you put a hard-to-catch horse in the same field with an easy-to-catch horse, most of the time you end up with two hard-to-catch horses. When you put a healthy child in the same room with a sick child most likely you will end up with two sick children. In other words, to be great, we must "hang out" with the great ones. We must set personal high expectations to seek out good, clean, pure, powerful, positive, productive individuals who make us better when they are around. On an organizational level: We cannot afford to have even one hard-to-catch, sick, negative employee around to contaminate and influence the healthy, positive employees. Negative cancer spreads and must be cut out. On the positive side, the highest organizational expectation is to have everybody keep their promises. When we hire people who keep their promises, this positive integrity spreads into the lives and habits of others. We don't worry about their taking extra time during breaks and lunch time or taking sick days when they are not sick. We expect them to meet commitments and to perform under pressure. They keep their promises - end of discussion! We must remember that *Total Customer Delight* means just that - total commitment from every employee to create *Delightful* results for the total list of customers.

3) **BE BRILLIANT AT TREATING YOUR EMPLOY-EES THE WAY YOU WANT YOUR CUSTOM-ERS TO BE TREATED.** If you take care of your employees it is almost guaranteed that your employees will take care of the customers. In sales, we call this "*Psychological Reciprocity*." When we make someone feel intelligent, important, appreciated, and needed during a sale, in a conversation, interview or appointment, it automatically creates a subconscious moral obligation for that person to immediately do all they know how to do to make us or another person they come in contact with feel equally intelligent, important, needed, and appreciated. If we are implicitly honest and consistent in our dealings with our em-

ployees, treating them not as subordinates but as respected co-workers, they trust us and want to be trusted. When we are fair with employees, they will be fair with customers. If we take time to write a special thank you (you can't re-read a conversation), send each employee a birthday card, anniversary card, acknowledge their children's birthday's, sympathize over family tragedies and support them in their extra curricular activities, they in turn will see the value in getting to know their customers on the same personal, intimate level and will acknowledge their important occasions. We must remember that people like to do business with winners and we like to do business with our friends. To create customer delight, we must make ourselves winners and friends!

4) **BE BRILLIANT AT EMPOWERING OTHERS WITH AN OWNERS MENTALITY.** In college we trashed our *Rented* dorm rooms and *Rented* apartments. The walls were dotted with picture hanging nail holes and the carpet changed colors with each new weekend party stain. We drive our rental cars harder than our own cars and even take them off-road over curbs and streams to places we wouldn't drive an M-1 tank. When was the last time we washed a rental car or changed its' oil? On the other hand, when we *Own* something, we take pride in the way it looks and performs. We baby it and think not only about short term benefits, but long term results. Ownership comes when we answer

three questions: Why should I? What's in it for me? Will it make me feel wanted and important? Ownership is passed along as we explain "why" we do something, relating it to what is important to the person we are empowering - i.e., service, charity, peace, environment, money, relationships, power, unconditional love. By explaining the intricate "why's" behind performance and productivity, we empower our co-workers to take personal responsibility for their actions and consequences. In this way, they become their own personal motivational speaker and they start working harder and smarter for the right reasons. Their performance is strong when we are around, and more importantly when we are not around. They stop passing the proverbial buck, they take ownership of each customer complaint, look at each problem as a challenge that they can solve and they serve the customer not because we say so, but because THEY SAY SO. Ownership makes it important for them to create customer delight.

5) **BE BRILLIANT AT INCREASING THE FREQUENCY OF FEEDBACK.** Feedback measurement is the breakfast of champions. It determines direction and destination. When NASA shoots a rocket into space, feedback determines its direction and destination. The second it goes off course, feedback kicks in and straightens its direction. Question: What would happen if we waited 60 to 90 days to check up on the

rocket like we do in business with our performance reviews? It would never reach its desired result. We must increase our frequency of feedback in our personal and professional lives. Feedback allows us to change our behavior before it is too late. It also allows us to pick the most appropriate behavior to keep the original dream, direction and commitment alive. When we do something and then report it back to a superior with full accountability, performance always improves! Track your customer service agent calls by monitoring their conversations. Grade and reward their proactive or reactive responses. If they are sub-par, refer back to the first four principles and practices listed in this essay to see if you missed something (maybe you simply hired the wrong person?). If not, proceed by teaching the most powerful customer service principle of all - Get it right the first time. Remember, "it's better to build a fence at the edge of the cliff than to park an ambulance at it's base."

6) **BE BRILLIANT AT SERVICE ABOVE SELF.** Getting it right the first time is no accident. It consistently comes when we empathetically put ourselves in the shoes of each customer and unconditionally serve and support them. To illustrate: A little girl was walking out the front door when her mother reminded her to come home immediately after school. The time to be home came and passed. Thirty minutes late, the girl finally walked in. "Where have you been? I've

been worried sick!" her mother scolded. "Oh Mommy. I was walking with my friend Sally and she dropped her doll and it broke all to pieces. It was just awful!" Her mother asked, "So you were late because you stayed to help Sally pick up the pieces and put the doll back together?" "Oh no mommy," her daughter replied. "I didn't know how to fix the doll, I just stayed to help her cry."

Yes, creating customer delight is a natural extension of hiring the right person, setting high expectations, treating employees like you want them to treat the customers, empowering them with authority to make decisions, increasing the frequency of feedback and living life with service above self. Creating *Customer Delight* truly is everybody's business.

DAN CLARK, CSP

Dan Clark, C.S.P. - Certified Speaking Professional, is one of the "hottest" speakers on the platform today. Since 1982, Dan has spoken to over two million people in all 50 states, throughout Canada, and in 11 other countries in Europe, Asia, and Russia.

Dan is the author of seven highly acclaimed books including "Getting High - How to Really Do It," "Puppies For Sale" (translated into Japanese and Russian), and "The Art of Being Alive." Dan is also a primary contributing author to the New York Times Best Sellers, "Chicken Soup for the Soul."

Dan is a successful businessman, actor, songwriter/recording artist, creator of over 40 audio and video training programs, and an award winning athlete who fought his way back from a paralyzing injury that cut short his football career.

Dan's client list is a Who's Who of the best organizations in the world including Meeting Professionals International, IBM, 3M, AT&T, Lucent Technologies, Boeing, ServiceMaster, Marriott Hotels, Nations Bank, Nordstrom, Prudential Insurance, Intermountain Health Care, Footlocker, the NCAA, the United Nations and hundreds more!

DAN CLARK, C.S.P.
Certified Speaking Professional
P.O. Box 8689
Salt Lake City, UT 84108

1-800-676-1121• 801-485-5755 • Fax 801-485-5789
Email sdanclarkp@aol.com

OTHER PRODUCTS

BOOKS

"The Art of Being Alive" .... $16.95 U.S.
(hard cover)
A parable revealing the 12 Precepts of the Art of Being Alive: Find a Mentor/Wizard, Live on Purpose, Create Mutual Respect and Support, Be True to Self, Keep Swinging, Communicate, Act-As-If, Increase Frequency of Feedback, Focus on Fundamentals, Expect Happiness, Manage Your Relationships and Follow the Final Formula. A must read book on Leadership, Empowerment and Personal Development relating to Management, Sales and Customer Service.

"Puppies For Sale" .... $12.95 U.S.
(soft cover - translated into Japanese and Russian)
This title comes from the tremendous popularity of one of Dan's many stories in the New York Times Best Sellers, "Chicken Soup For The Soul." This is Dan's own sequel collection of over 200 inspirational stories that will hug your heart and snuggle your soul. A perfect resource for speeches and articles.

"Getting High - How To Really Do It" .... $10.95U.S.
(soft cover)
Twelve chapters written especially for teenagers in language and stories they can understand. Motivation, Respect for Authority, Inspiration, Attitude, Goal Setting, Stay in School, Drug Prevention, Suicide Solution and Patriotism.

AUDIO TAPES

"The Art of Being Alive" .... $99.95 U.S.
A comprehensive series encompassing Dan's unique approach to life, personal and professional relationships, parenting, coaching and teaching. Dan discusses the 12 precepts of the Art of Being Alive. *12 audio cassettes recorded live with commentaries in the studio.*

"The Art of Relationship Management" .... $19.95 U.S.
Fundamental customer service concerns and advanced sales techniques that will give you the competitive advantage, increase sales, create customer delight, and positively effect your bottom line. *2 audio cassettes recorded live!*

"The Art of Empowerment" .... $19.95 U.S.
Effective leadership always comes from the inside out. Learn that control is only an illusion - learn the difference between inspiration and motivation, leadership and management; learn teambuilding skills from someone who actually played on a team; create a winning organization. *2 audio cassettes recorded live!*

"The Art of Teaching" .... $19.95 U.S.
Dan believes teaching is the profession that makes all other professions possible. A program especially for K-12 teachers, school support staff, secretaries, food service, transportation and custodians - everyone who is involved in the educational arena. *A 1½ hour in-service recorded live! 2 audio cassettes.*

Please included $5.00 U.S. shipping and handling • Mastercard and Visa welcome.
For a complete catalog of Dan's books, audio and video learning systems, music albums, t-shirts and posters, as well as information on Dan's keynote speeches and seminars, please contact Dan at:

Dan Clark & Associates

P.O. Box 8689 - Salt Lake City, UT 84108
1-800-676-1121, 801-485-5755, Fax 801-485-5789,
Email sdanclarkp@aol.com

Only The BEST

BRAVO!!!

BUILDING A BLOCK-BUSTER RETAIL BUSINESS WITH SHOW-STOPPING CUSTOMER SERVICE

MARC HARDY

CUSTOMER SERVICE

Bravo!!!

Building A Block-Buster Retail Business With Show-Stopping Customer Service

Marc Hardy

Building a retail business is a lot like producing a play. You have to present something that people are willing to leave their homes and pay for; it must be well advertised; you should have adequate parking; the facilities should set the mood; the players should be well rehearsed; and you as playwright, producer and director must work with many others to pull the show together so that people will come back again and again. After all, the opinion of critics will make or break your run at success.

Business is theatre, especially in customer service and sales, two areas that really are not separate from one another. Like the lyrics and melody of a song from a Broadway musical, they appeal much more if they are in sync with each other. So it is with inside sales and customer service, where your opportunity for sales is limited by the number of customers that enter your "theatre." Once they are there, it is up to you to make sure they have a pleasant experience and return again, hopefully with friends and family.

Start With A Good Script

During my tenure as a jewelry store manager in a low traffic mall, I conceived a script titled "Customer Obsessed" and used it in my store. After three years the store had the largest sales percentage increase in the entire thirty three store chain - all because of great customer service. In an economy that is evolving into discount mega-stores for almost everything, a medium sized business cannot compete on price. Nor can they compete with merely good customer service - even giant Wal-Mart has pleasant greeters - they must have great customer service. But the larger the giants get the more vulnerable they become because they start believing policies are more important than the needs of the customer, or as they say in television, they become "bigger than the series." They let their egos get in the way, stop using the lines from the old script and make up new ones that serve their interests better than those of their audience.

An instance of this happened a few years ago when I bought a $12 item from Wal-Mart and wrote a check. The item was not what I needed so I returned it the next day, only to be told that I would have to wait three days until my check cleared before I could get a refund. This meant I would have to take another hour out of my day to return to get MY money. I was not only incensed that they didn't care about the inconvenience they had caused me, but their policy also inferred that my check may not be any good and I was the kind of person that would rip them off for $12. However, the customer service clerk was adamant, stating it was company policy.

The problem was not the clerk. The problem was that the company had written some bad lines in the script for her to present to the customer. She had learned her lines well and evidently was informed by the left-brained playwrights that there would be absolutely no ad-libbing. Flexibility was not an option, and she did not satisfy the questions of this particular heckler and critic.

As customers we are in essence critics; we are all qualified to say good things or bad things about those to whom we pay money for services. Wanting to help them improve their chances for a long run, I wrote a long letter to the president of Wal-Mart, to which no one responded. Not a word. Not even a vice-president or assistant. No one really cared. Perhaps my $12 purchase was considered the same as a cheap seat in the peanut gallery. As a result, I have not stepped foot inside a Wal-Mart store and you, like thousands of people, are reading this account of their aloofness. Sound like sour grapes on my part? You betcha! But how many of Wal-Mart's customers have had the same experience and the same response?

Don't write scripts for your employees that don't serve the interests of the paying public. In fact, why not promote your show by advertising that customers don't have to wait three days for their check to clear at your store? Let customers know that you value their time and have faith in their character, that you want their experience with you to have a happy ending.

Choosing the Cast and Rehearsal

Disney is legendary for calling their employees "cast members." They know how important each person's part is in their overall success. The cast members must reflect the kind of image you want to project and even great actors are not right for every part. So be picky about who you hire.

Next, make sure they have the kind of background knowledge for the part and that they look credible. You wouldn't have a ten year old child play an eighty year old man . Not only would the child not be physically right, but he would not have the knowledge of how an older man might move or speak. So make sure your employees have the knowledge and experience to play the part.

That's why I now purchase my home improvement items from the local hardware store at a little higher price and a lot less hassle. The hardware store personnel are knowledgeable about fixing things and have helped me avoid purchasing the wrong item for the job in the first place. I have learned that the price you pay for good advice is worth its weight in gold. It saves you time, frustration and in the long term, money. But the best part? They know me by name and greet me like an old friend. They play their roles well. No discount in the world can give you that kind of personal satisfaction.

The worst mistake any director can make is to assume the actors will learn their lines and know how to act on their own. If that were true, directors and managers wouldn't be needed. Rehearse your people over and over until they get it right. The more they rehearse the more natural they become in their parts and the more they and the customer will enjoy the encounter. If they complain that acting is fake, ask them if they think their favorite actors and actresses are fake. Good actors take the best of who they are and magnify those qualities.

Appropriate Costumes and Make-Up

When I was in the jewelry business, people would come into my store looking for a job dressed and accessorized in creative ways. Often they wore dirty T-shirts, torn jeans, a three day growth on their face, orange hair, lime green polyester leisure suits, earrings in their eye brows or tongues, spandex jogging suits - you get the idea. These eclectic attires might work in a rock music store, a pawn shop or a gym, but they are not the right costume for a jewelry store.

Remember: the audience is not there for the amusement of the actors - the actors are there for the enjoyment of the audience. If you are going to perform in a hardware store, three inch heels are not the costume of choice, however they might be in a women's clothing store. You must decide the correct attire for your play and enforce it - nothing looks stranger than Shakespearean actors in period costumes with Romeo in Dockers and Juliet in a Guess sweat shirt. It may make a personal statement, but it detracts from the larger, more important task of giving the audience what they paid to see.

Make-up and accessories are just as important. Do you want your players to have five earrings in one ear, purple hair and black lipstick? Maybe, if you own a Halloween shop. Do tattoos on women offend you or your patrons? Maybe, unless you own a biker's bar and/or a tattoo parlor. Are dirty hands and face acceptable? In a car repair shop yes, in a jewelry store, no. All of this is an important part of the effect you are trying to achieve.

Impressive Set Design

In what setting does your play take place? Is your store dark and dreary? Are the shelves filthy, and are there finger prints all over the windows? Is the tan carpet so dirty it is now calico? Is the floor vacuumed and swept?

Are your bathrooms untidy (my personal litmus test of a well run operation) and do you let customers use them? Are your displays neat and organized or do people feel confused as soon as they walk through the door?

Ambiance is everything when it comes to first impressions. Set designers in the theatre know that color and lighting can make or break a scene and that the set itself sets the tone for the entire experience. Appearance is often a reflection of the business philosophy of the manager or owner. If a store is dirty and disorganized it speaks volumes about management's attitude toward their customers - they don't really care what we think. If they did they would get their act together and wow us with their best stuff. Before you open the curtain on your business every morning, make sure the set is ready to wow the audience.

Promotion Through People

Okay. Now you have written your blockbuster script, hired the right actors, rehearsed their lines, picked the costumes, designed the set...now will anyone show up? Use your actors to spread the word about your business. If they take pride in their role they will tell everyone what a great place it is to work . How many times do you hear that from people?

If you are going to promote your store based on great

customer service and a shopping experience that commands a standing ovation, then do what the movie producers do. In every commercial, let your customers talk about how great you are. Interview them, get quotes from them, cultivate them because their comments carry far more weight with potential customers than yours. Plus, you make them one of the stars of your show and they become celebrities! And best of all, their endorsement costs you nothing.

People telling other people is how block-buster movies become successful. A "Two Thumbs Up!" from Siskel and Ebert is worth more than a multi-million dollar advertising budget. "Waterworld" had a tremendous budget but was felled by the spoken word. On the other hand the sleeper movie "Rocky" became a smash success because people convinced others that they just <u>had</u> to see it. Why not follow their example and avoid wasting tons of money on ineffective sales pitches. Let your customers be your public relations firm and your sales force - for free!

<u>Opening Night</u>

Everyday is opening night. Any actor will tell you that when they are no longer nervous about going on stage they do not do their best work. They work hard at not resting on their laurels because the audience doesn't care how good they were the night before - they paid for <u>this</u> night. And they deserve the best performance the actor can give. Don't disappoint them and they will guarantee your success for a long run.

The Secret To A Long Run...

...is consistency. Actors and employees will come and go and products and plays will change, but the knowledge that customers' expectations will always be met or exceeded is what keeps people coming back and telling others about you. Just as you should never mount a show that is not ready, you should not offer something you cannot deliver or present an inferior product. These short-sighted efforts always come back to haunt you in the long term, no matter how much money is made in the short term.

The reason famous actors, actresses, directors and producers are successful and have box office draw is because audiences know that they consistently deliver what people expect. Frank Capra produces movies with happy endings, Mel Brooks, Steve Martin and Woopie Goldberg deliver comedy, Steven Cannell delivers hit TV shows, and Clint Eastwood delivers excitement and intensity. They all have their own style but they all deliver what the audience is willing to pay for. Customers come because you have established a certain standard. Anything less than that standard is called a "bomb." Anything above the standard is a "showstopper!" So write your script, rehearse your play, create your reality and break a leg!

MARC HARDY

As a speaker and author, Marc Hardy's humorous insights on the adversity we encounter in our professional and personal lives have been enjoyed by thousands of people throughout the United States and Canada.

Thought provoking and funny, he redefines the meaning of failure and making mistakes, treating them not as obstacles to success but necessary steps toward success. He draws on his experience in management in profit and not-for-profit organizations for the past 20 years in more than a dozen industries; he has work in construction, factories, jewelry stores, bakeries, and professional theatre.

He served as a reserve police officer and was chosen "Reserve Recruit of the Year", and for seven years was the executive director of a private foundation and think tank.

His degree in Human Resources Management and his diverse background allow him to relate to almost any audience. He has received several awards for outstanding sales and in 1991 was voted one of the top three speakers in the "World Championship of Public Speaking". His articles have appeared in several publications including Bottom Line Business, The American Salesman, Human Resource Professional, Employee Services Management, Business Opportunities Journal, and Mid-America Commerce and Industry, and he is a co-author of Only The Best on Leadership published by WIN Publications.

Programs:

Keynotes:

*"**Daring Greatly:** How to value adversity, look forward to failure and make our mistakes meaningful"*

*"**Smooth Stones, Broken Bones And Danger Zones:** Wit and Wisdom from Life's School of Hard Knocks"*

Workshops:

*"**Creating Leadership Teams:** A Workshop for Not-For-Profit Board Directors, Managers and Employees"*

*"**Unlimited Influence:** Powerful Presentation Secrets of Professional Speakers and Trainers"*

OTHER PRODUCTS

Audio Tapes:

"Daring Greatly" (One hour Keynote) $10.00

"Unlimited Influence" (Three tape set) $30.00

"Articles On Tape" $10.00

Books:

"Only The Best On Leadership" $11.95

*For information on all Marc's products, or for information
regarding speaking engagements, please contact:*

Marc Hardy & Associates
58485 Hilly Lane
Elkhart, Indiana 46517-2241
219-295-7600 • 800-850-6509
Fax: 219-522-3355

Only The **BEST**

IT'S NOT ROCKET SCIENCE!

LARRY WINGET

CUSTOMER SERVICE

IT'S NOT ROCKET SCIENCE!

LARRY WINGET

Customer Service is not hard. Got it? It is not hard. It is simple. We have made it hard. Harder than it has to be and harder than it should be. We have made customer service all about techniques, processes and how-to's when customer service is really about a handful of simple principles. Go to the seminars and read the books and listen to the tapes and watch the videos; it can't hurt. In fact, in most cases it will help. But understand this, without this handful of simple principles to build a foundation upon, all of the training in the world will only provide a temporary fix and build organizations full of little customer service robots with strained smiles and superficial, insincere pleasantness.

Offended? Sorry. But there is no reason for this to be such a big deal. Simplify your approach to customer service by adopting these simple principles for customer service success.

Motive.

> Customer service is more about why
> we do our jobs than how we do our jobs.

Why do most people go to work every single day? Well, here is the most common answer: to make money. In my opinion that's a lousy reason to go to work. I have found that the faster we chase money, the faster it runs away. Instead, it is important to remember that money is the result of our service. The more we serve others, the more they will reward us with their business and their cash.

> The more we serve others,
> the more they will reward us
> with their business and their cash.

Take responsibility.

For everything. Don't assume that someone else has greeted the customer, or thanked the customer, or offered to help the customer or apologized to the customer. And since I just mentioned the word "apologize," let me expound further. Say you are sorry. Say you are sorry for stuff you didn't even do. Be sorry for anything that goes wrong and everything that goes wrong.

Can you imagine what it would be like to be a customer at a business where every employee took personal responsibility for the success of the organization? The place would be spotless, because everyone would pick up after themselves and each other. No more, "It's not my job!" Instead, everyone would say, "You bet it's my job!" Then every employee would greet you, say it was good to see you, offer to help you, make sure you were happy and satisfied, and thank you for shopping with them. What would you then do in return? You would rush out to tell the world how great this place was to do business with. You would be so impressed that every person you came in contact with would have to hear about the amazing experience you had with them. And then they would go and experience the same thing, and then they would tell others and then they would go and . . . (can you see where this might be a good thing?)

One person really *can* make the difference. An organization can have the best product, the best location, the best pricing, the best of everything and one employee with a bad attitude can say one stupid thing and ruin it all. On the other hand, a company can be marginal in most areas and have a customer focused employee who takes responsibility and the results can be amazing. People still do business with people, and people who learn to take personal responsibility for making every customer happy will always be successful.

> Take personal responsibility for
> making every customer happy.

Keep your word.

Do exactly what you say are going to do, when you say you are going to do it, the way you said it was going to be done. The only appropriate surprise for customers is the surprise that comes when you have done everything they expect and then some.

Be nice.

Being nice is not a technique. It's a principle. Being nice to customers comes from being a nice person. It is impossible for a mean person to be nice. Here is a clue: only hire nice people. It saves so much time, money, effort and frustration. Remember this:

> A jerk with a bunch of
> customer service techniques
> under his belt is still a jerk!

Be flexible.

Policies and procedures are important, but not as important as customers. Learn to be flexible. We must be flexible about how we do our job, – the process, – and inflexible about why we do our job,– the purpose. Our purpose is to serve; the way we do it should be flexible enough to accommodate the customer. Our purpose will never change, but how we do it must change. Let me tell you a quick story about a couple of employees who had no idea about the difference between process and purpose.

One day while shopping in a mall with my two sons, I realized that I needed to buy some batteries. I spotted a store that I knew sold batteries. I am not going to tell you the name of the store, but I will tell you that their first product was probably a radio and they probably started in a shack some place. Upon entering the store, I saw batteries hanging on the wall. I pulled them off the wall and placed them on the counter along with enough cash to pay for them.

At that point, a young man approached the other side of the counter, looked at the batteries, looked at my money, looked and my sons and me and says, "Could I have your name, address, and telephone number?" I answered with "No." He said, "I have to have your name, address, and telephone number in order to sell you the batteries." I told him that wasn't going to happen and asked him why it was so important for him to have that information. That is when he told me the number one thing that no customer ever wants to hear; he told me that is was Company Policy. I informed him that I had a Customer Policy that said when I was paying cash, I didn't have to tell him who I was. He immediately reached across the counter and pushed the batteries away and said, "Sir, we aren't going to be able to do business with you." I was amazed and asked him if there was a manager around. He said that he would go in the back and get him.

In a moment, a guy who I recognized right off to be a manager (a kid about nineteen) came walking down the aisle with his finger pointed at me. When he got right in front of me, he pointed his finger right at my face and said "Bud, do you have a problem?" I said, "No I don't have a problem, you have batteries and I have money. In America, that makes a deal." He then told me that he had to have my name, address and telephone number in order to sell me the batteries. I explained that his employee had already explained that to me and that I wasn't going to do it. I then asked him why it was so important. That is when he told me the number two thing that no customer ever wants to hear. He said it was because that is the way that had ALWAYS done it. I told him I had good news for him. Today he was going to get a chance to do it different. That was when he pushed the batteries away again and told me they weren't going to do business with me.

As he started to walk away, I suggested that he stop and think about it before he walked away from me. He stopped, and after several seconds turned back to his computer and began to type. Then he put the batteries in a sack, put my money in the drawer, put a receipt in the sack and handed it to me. I asked him what he did. He said, "I figured it out. I just my own name, address and telephone number on your receipt."

No brain surgeon here. This guy had an unhappy customer walking out his front door, but now I had his name, address, and telephone number. Here was a company who had done an excellent job in training its people in policies and procedures . . . the process. But they had never gotten across to them that their reason for being there every moment of every single day was to serve customers . . . the purpose.

Be proactive.

The attitude you approach the customer with is pretty much the attitude you can expect from them in return. The key to dealing with other people is to set an example for them to follow. When we take a proactive approach and begin every relationship with a smile, a friendly face and an attitude of willingness to help the customer, it is more likely that we will get a positive response from the customer. So take the lead.

> We must become the kind of
> person we want our customers to be.

Love what you do.

When you love what you do, you will figure out a way to be good at it. Excellence and quality have been beaten to death in the past few years. I think that we should focus on finding people who love what they do or at least helping people to love what they do. When we love what we do we will naturally search out ways to be excellent at it. And the converse is that it is impossible to be excellent at something you don't like doing.

> When we love what we do we will
> naturally search out ways to be excellent at it.

Be fun.

People are attracted to places and people that are fun to do business with.

> Have fun at what you do and others will
> have fun spending their money with you.

Never turn back.

This is an ongoing process. You can't do this stuff for a while and then let it slide. That is what happens to people and organizations who learn the techniques and don't have the principles upon which to build their foundation. Techniques can be forgotten, but principles develop into a lifestyle that lasts.

Remember:

We always get referrals. When we mess up, the customer tells other people. When we do good, the customer tells other people. We get to determine the kind of stories that our customer is going to tell.

Our customers have all the money. We have to serve them, be nice to them, help them and appreciate them in order to get them to share their money with us willingly.

> All of the money you are ever going to have
> is currently in the hands of someone else.
> Earl Nightingale

See? I told you it wasn't rocket science!

It really isn't hard now is it? It simply comes down to a few simple principles that anyone can use regardless of their job or industry. Look again. No techniques. No fancy ideas. Just plain common sense for treating people in such a way that they will share their money with us willingly and enjoy doing it.

LARRY WINGET, CSP

Larry Winget began life on a chicken ranch in Muskogee, Oklahoma. He has driven a bookmobile and was one of the first male telephone operators in the Bell System. He has shoveled manure, swept floors, sold, managed, and been the company president. He has experienced both incredible business success and total business failure. However, he is proof that you can go belly-up in business without going face down in failure.

Larry is currently an internationally recognized speaker and seminar leader. He is the author of more than a dozen books and the creator of many audio/video learning systems, as well as lots of other unique personal development products.

Larry is an active member of the National Speakers Association, a charter member of the Oklahoma Speakers Association, and a Certified Speaking Professional (CSP).

He speaks on the subjects of Success, Leadership, Teambuilding, Being Customer Obsessed, and Prosperity. He is also widely known as a humorist and all 'round funny guy. Regardless of the topic, you can be assured that his material is centered around universal principles that will work for anyone, at any time, and in any business. Plus, Larry reads over one hundred books per year to make sure that his stuff is current and that he knows what he's talking about.

Larry believes that success in either our personal or professional life is not hard. It simply comes down to knowing what to do and doing it. He is committed to helping everyone understand that they deserve the best and can have it, when they follow a few simple principles. Known for his unique style, Larry's down-to-earth, humorous, bottom-line approach makes his "stuff" fresh, fun, and easy to implement.

Larry Winget has discovered his uniqueness and learned to exploit it in the service of others. His symbol is the exclamation point. His heroes are Tarzan, Superman, and The Lone Ranger. His dogs are Elvis and Nixon. His wife is Rose Mary. His boys, Tyler and Patrick. His philosophy is, "Expect the best. Be prepared for the worst. Celebrate it all!"

ORDER FORM

For Fastest Service
Call TOLL-FREE
1-800-749-4597
10:00 am - 3:00 pm, weekdays, CST

24 Hour Fax Line
918-747-3185

W I N   S E M I N A R S !

1232 E. 25th St, TULSA OK 74114

QUANTITY DISCOUNTS

Are available on all of
Larry's STUFF.
Call for details.

For Seminar Information Call:
1-800-749-4597
1-918-745-6606

SHIPPING & HANDLING WITHIN USA

If Sub Total amount is:
0 - 25.00..$ 3.00
25.01 - 100.00 ....$ 6.00
100.01 - 200.00................................$10.00
200.01 - 300.00................................$12.00

Call for rates on purchases over $300.

SHIPPING & HANDLING TO CANADA

If Sub Total amount is:
0 - 25.00..$ 5.00
25.01 - 100.00 ....$ 8.00
100.01 - 200.00................................$12.00
200.01 - 300.00................................$15.00

Call for rates on purchases over $300.

Rates do not include duty, taxes or customs
charges that COULD be charged
at the border

Larry's Stuff

	Unit Cost	Quantity	Amount
Books			
The Simple Way To Success...$12.95		____	_____
Money Stuff.............................,..$11.95		____	_____
Stuff That Works Every Single Day .... ,.......................$ 9.95		____	_____
The Little Red Book Of Stuff That Works ....$ 7.95		____	_____
Just Do This Stuff ....$ 7.95		____	_____
101 Things That Make You Say UNGAWA! ....$ 5.95		____	_____
Only The Best On Success..$11.95		____	_____
Only The Best On Customer Service.......................................$11.95		____	_____
Only The Best On Leadership $11.95		____	_____
Profound Stuff...$ 9.95		____	_____
Larry's Library (all TEN above)..$80.00		____	_____
Audio			
Larry – LIVE!...$ 9.95		____	_____
Video			
Simple Way To Success $39.95		____	_____
We're All In This Together $39.95		____	_____
Learning Systems			
How To Get Booked And Make Money- FAST!...(4 audios) $39.95		____	_____
Other Stuff			
How To Write A Book ...*Book*...$ 11.95		____	_____
Exclamation Point (!) *pin*...$ 5.00		____	_____
UNGAWA! *coffee mug*...$ 8.95		____	_____
Shut Up, Stop Whining And Get A Life *coffee mug*................$ 8.95		____	_____
Winning Words Mini-Posters $17.95		____	_____
Stuff That Works Every Single Day (50)...................................$ 9.95		____	_____
The Three Reasons We Are Here (50).....................................$ 9.95		____	_____
Pat On The Back (50) ....$ 9.95		____	_____
Ten Commandments For Being Customer Focused (50)...........$ 9.95		____	_____
This Day (50)...$ 9.95		____	_____
Money Stuff Affirmation Cards (50)..$ 9.95		____	_____
Thanks Cards (100)...$ 9.95		____	_____
Expect The Best Poster, Framed...$12.95		____	_____
UNGAWA GEAR			
UNGAWA! *T-shirt (XL or XXL)*..$17.95		____	_____
No Doubts Allowed *T-shirt (XL or XXL)*.................................$17.95		____	_____
Customers Are Everything *T-shirt (XL or XXL)*.......................$17.95		____	_____
Shut Up, Stop Whining And Get A Life *T-shirt (XL or XXL)* $17.95		____	_____
Larry – World Tour *T-shirt (XL or XXL)*...................................$17.95		____	_____
Shut Up, Stop Whining And Get A Life *hat*............................$16.95		____	_____

Sub Total _____

Please use chart at left for figuring **Shipping & Handling** _____

TOTAL _____

Name _____ Date _____

Company _____

STREET Address _____

City/Province _____

Zip/Postal Code _____ Country _____ Day Phone _____

Method of Payment: ☐ VISA   ☐ Mastercard   ☐ Check/Money Order Enclosed

Card No. / / / / / / / / / / / / / / / / / / /

Exp. date _____ Signature _____